THE LEVELLERS
AND THE
ENGLISH REVOLUTION

THE LEVELLERS

AND THE

ENGLISH REVOLUTION

by

HENRY HOLORENSHAW

with a Foreword by

JOSEPH NEEDHAM

NEW YORK

Howard Fertig

1971

First published in 1939

HOWARD FERTIG, INC. EDITION 1971
published by arrangement with the author

Library of Congress Catalog Card Number: 73-80559

FOR
STAN, LILY,
GEORGE AND SONIA,
THIS STORY OF WHAT
THE ENGLISH DID

PRINTED IN THE UNITED STATES OF AMERICA
BY NOBLE OFFSET PRINTERS, INC.

FOREWORD

By JOSEPH NEEDHAM

It is a particular pleasure to me to write a short introduction to the little book of my friend, Mr. Holorenshaw, for my work in the history of science has shown me that the story of man's intellectual progress cannot be understood save in the light of his social progress. It is no coincidence that the great re-birth of experimental science in Europe and in England at the end of the seventeenth century took place in a revolutionary period during and after a civil war (our English Revolution, 1642–50) in which one economic system, feudalism, perished, and another, capitalism, came to its modern stature. Weber and Tawney have shown us how puritanism was the accompaniment of the rising class of capitalist merchants. Merton has shown how puritan were the early Fellows of the Royal Society.

But if human social progress always takes place by means of revolutions, they nevertheless go on the principle of two steps forward and one step back. Mr. Holorenshaw here for the first time brings information together about the most advanced spirits in our English Revolution, those who, several centuries in advance of their time, under the name of Levellers and Diggers, wished not only for freedom to exploit and trade, but for the freedom of equals in joint ownership—in a word, for Socialism, two hundred years before that word was coined. And Mr. Holorenshaw points out that no less than the men of property, the Levellers realised the social importance of science, and foresaw the part it would one day play in human welfare. Lastly, he shows, and it is of much importance to-day, that the leaders of the socialists of Cromwell's time were true-born English-men every one, and indeed that it was in England, our England of the game-laws and the factory children, that men first saw the vision of the co-operative social com-monwealth, where the iniquity of class should for ever be swept away.

CONTENTS

A Selection of

DRAMATIS PERSONÆ

Mr. Oliver Cromwell, Lieut.-General; later Lord Protector of the Commonwealth of England.

Lord Fairfax, General of the Parliamentary forces.

Commissary-General Henry Ireton, son-in-law to Oliver Cromwell.

Major-General Thomas Harrison
Major-General Edmund Ludlow } Republicans.
Colonel Alured
Sir Arthur Haslerig

Cornet Joyce, captor of the King.

Colonel Pride, purgator of the House.

Mr. Berry
Mr. Swallow } Captains of Colonel Cromwell's troops
Mr. Margery of horse.

Mr. John Milton, Latin Secretary to the Commonwealth of England and leader-writer of *Mercurius Politicus.*

Mr. M. Needham, Editor of *Mercurius Politicus.*

Corporal Church
Corporal Perkins } of Colonel Whalley's
Cornet Thompson regiment.

LEADERS OF THE LEVELLERS:

Lieut.-Colonel John Lilburne (" Freeborn John ").

Mr. Gerrard Winstanley, Digger.

Master Wm. Walwyn, of the City of London.

Mr. Rich. Overton.

Colonel Thomas Rainborough, later Admiral of the Fleet.

Major Edward Sexby.

Major Wildman (" John Lawmind ").

Major Cobbett of Snow Hill.

Captain Thompson.

Mr. Robert Everard, Agitator of Lieut.-General Cromwell's regiment.

Mr. William Everard, Digger.

Mr. William Russell, Agitator of Colonel Whalley's regiment.

Lieutenant Richard Rumbold.

Mr. Robert Lockyer
Mr. Richard Arnold } Troopers.

Mr. William Larner, printer
Mr. Giles Calvert, publisher } to the Levellers in London.

Mr. William Dell, sometime Chaplain (Independent) to the New Model Army and later Master of Caius College in Cambridge.

Mr. John Goodwin, Independent Minister of Coleman Street Chapel, London.

Mr. Clement Walker ⎱ Presbyterian Ministers; no friends to the
Mr. Thomas Edwards ⎰ Army.

Mr. John Bunyan, tinker, private in the Parliamentary garrison of Newport Pagnell.

The Hon. Robert Boyle ⎫
Dr. John Wilkins   ⎬ members of the Invisible College.
Dr. Thomas Willis   ⎭

Mr. Peter Chamberlain, friend to the poor   ⎫
Mr. Samuel Hartlib, friend to Comenius   ⎬ writers.
Mr. John Cook, Solicitor-General at the King's trial ⎭

Mr. Almond ⎱ members of the Cambridge Committee of the
Mr. Spalding ⎰ Eastern Counties Association.

NOTE. The term " English Revolution " has usually been applied to the changes of 1688–9, when the Stuart dynasty was replaced by William of Orange; but it would be much better to reserve it, as in this book, for the Civil War period 1642–50 which is analogous with the French Revolution.

CHAPTER I

INTRODUCTION : WHO *WERE* THE LEVELLERS?

THE ENGLISH CIVIL WAR

ENGLISHMEN MAY BE FORGIVEN if they study seven-teenth century England with special enthusiasm. It was a period of fundamental changes; it saw the true transi-tion from the Middle Ages to the modern world, the beginning of modern science, and the end of religious autocracy. English writing, deeply affected by these changes, reached heights, as in Milton and Browne, unknown before or since. In all historical processes there are certain particularly important turning-points, times when contradictions which previously had been latent, or which it had been possible to gloss over, can no longer be concealed and when nothing will mend the conflict except resort to the arbitrament of civil war. But the Civil War in England in the seventeenth century was only one aspect of a whole series of struggles which were going on throughout the century and which reached a definite settlement at its end. When we learn history at school, we hear about the battles of Cromwell, Prince Rupert, Newcastle and others, and we know that the execution of Charles I made England a Commonwealth until the revolution in 1660 brought back the monarchy in a second Stuart dynasty. But it all remains entirely enigmatic in the absence of a general interpretation. Now, the only interpretation which really illuminates the seventeenth century is arrived at when we begin to look at the economic changes which were then going on. The seventeenth century cannot be understood except by the realisation that a transition was taking place from the political power of the feudal aristocracy to that of the capitalist merchants. In other words, the Civil War was England's " *bourgeois* revolution." To the town merchants were allied the lesser country gentry, most of whom had no continuous connection with the Mediæval feudal landlords, and whose sons formed a considerable part of the City apprentices.

Of course, the history of capitalism goes back a very long time before the seventeenth century. The economic historians have traced it even into the twelfth century, and there is much reason for thinking that it first grew up in close connection with long-distance transport, especially shipping. If it was easy to determine, as the theologians liked to do, the just price of so many eggs brought in a few miles to a town market, it was not at all easy to decide what should be the just recompense for a cargo of wheat taken from Scandinavia to Spain at a time of famine in the latter country, in peril of sea-robbers and bad weather on the way. It could be sold for what it would fetch. By the seventeenth century enormous advances were being made in financial technique, such as the invention of cheques, etc. Moreover, men were beginning to realise that the new scientific methods of experiment and observation would bring about profound changes in industry. Hence we see the meaning of the insistence by seventeenth-century writers on the importance for trades and husbandry of the " new or experimental philosophy." All these progressive movements found themselves opposed by the forces of feudalism, headed by certain courts, of which England's was a notable example. Thus it came about that the first capitalists of the cities like Amsterdam, Antwerp and London in the seventeenth century formed a revolutionary group, and it was the London merchants, in alliance with the lesser country gentry, who formed England's new middle class. It is striking to recall that in the seventeenth century Englishmen were regarded throughout Europe, after 1649, with some such feelings of horror as Russians after 1917; for it was Englishmen, not Russians, who set the example in Europe of executing a king when his actions seemed to be clean contrary to the good of the people.

THE PARTIES IN THE ENGLISH REVOLUTION

If these interpretations of seventeenth-century England are roughly correct, we should expect to find what one might call a " left wing " of the revolutionary forces. In general, we do not sufficiently distinguish between the various groups which made up the Parliamentary strength against the King. It will be convenient if we enumerate some of these much as John Reed, in his *Ten Days that Shook the World* listed the political groups of the revolutionary Russia of 1917.

In making this list, it will be necessary to refer to religious groups as well as political ones, for in those days the distinction was by no means so clear as it is to-day.

On the one hand, there were the Royalists. They included Roman Catholics, Anglicans and Presbyterians. It would be a mistake to regard them as entirely on the reactionary side in social matters. For example, the Anglican bishops, especially men like Archbishop Laud, were really the representatives of Mediæval ideas of social justice. That is to say, they were opposed to the enclosure of the common lands by the rich landlords and they favoured a policy whereby the peasants, on the one hand, and the King, on the other, would be strengthened. It is important to note also that they were vigorously opposed to usury, although without some considerable weakening of the Mediæval prohibition against the taking of money upon interest, no form of capitalist economic system could grow up. The Royalist party was, of course, entirely monarchist, but a belief in the necessity of a monarch was not confined to them. Many of those on the Parliamentary side were opposed only to the Stuart monarchs, or even simply to Charlies I himself. As late as 1650, it was not obvious that all the Parliamentary leaders favoured a republican government. In fact, at the very end of the Commonwealth, it was possible for some of them to restore kingship without departing very much from their previously confessed opinion. But what is exceedingly important about the reformed constitutional monarchy at the end of the century is that it was representative of the interests of the city of London and the new middle class. It was a *bourgeois*, not an aristocratic, monarchy.

Turning now to the Parliamentary side of the Civil War. The two main divisions on the Parliamentary side were the Presbyterians and the Independents. We need not go into the difference between these parties in respect of Church government; what was characteristic of them was that, in general, the Presbyterians were conservative and the Independents were radical. But the Independents themselves were divided into the so-called " Gentlemen Independents," of whom Cromwell, Ireton, Fairfax and others were the most distinguished; and the more popular party, which was given the name of the " Levellers." The Levellers definitely represented the extreme left wing of the Parliamentary forces. They are passed by with hardly a mention in the orthodox history books of schools and colleges, although, as soon as one begins to read about them, one finds that they were—to judge from many of their leaders' writings— far in advance of their time. Moreover, their political strength was greater than is generally thought. In 1649 they were strong enough to take the field against Cromwell's own forces in a short campaign which nearly unseated him. The essential point about the Levellers was that they were men who were not content with the political equality which the Cromwellian system would give, but demanded a much greater measure of economic equality, so that England could be a Commonwealth in reality as well as in name. From 1648 onwards, the Parliamentary side split more and more into two parts, the main body, satisfied with the victory of the city of London over the feudal aristocracy, and a smaller body desirous of pushing on towards something nearer to modern ideas of a socialist state.

These relationships can be rather well expressed by means of the diagram on page 16.

Let us summarise the background to this diagram. Almost from the beginning of the century there had been going on a struggle against the feudal monarchy. This opposition took two outward forms, religious (the Puritan movement), and political (Parliament); but it had one inner meaning, the demand of the rising capitalist class, first for freedom and then for power. The religious opposition came to a head in the Edinburgh riots of 1637, the Presbyterian Covenant of 1638, and the war won by the Scottish Presbyterians in 1640. The political opposition centred round the disputed right of the King to levy taxes without the consent of Parliament (cf. the famous " Ship Money," 1634–6). By 1641 the exasperation of the parties led to an attempt on the part of the King to arrest five M.P.'s, which failed. In the following year there was a struggle for the control of the militia, the Navy declared for Parliament, and the King, after issuing Commissions of Array, set up his standard at Nottingham.

The first Civil War at first went badly for the Parliament, in spite of their victories at Edgehill (1642) and Marston Moor (1644). A whole expeditionary force had to surrender in Cornwall. But the organisation of the New Model Army changed the situation, won a decisive victory at Naseby (1645) and ended the war at Stow-on-the-Wold (1646). The King was now in captivity, the Army had become definitely revolutionary, in 1647

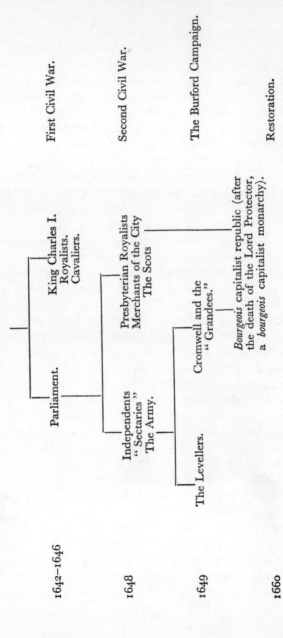

First Civil War.

Second Civil War.

The Burford Campaign.

Restoration.

King Charles I.
Royalists.
Cavaliers.

Presbyterian Royalists
Merchants of the City
The Scots

Bourgeois capitalist republic (after
the death of the Lord Protector,
a *bourgeois* capitalist monarchy).

Parliament.

Independents
" Sectaries "
The Army.

Cromwell and the
" Grandees."

The Levellers.

1642–1646

1648

1649

1660

Agitators were elected, and the break between Presbyterians and Independents grew wider. Next year the second Civil War broke out. Presbyterians united with Royalists, but were defeated at Maidstone and Colchester. This led to the trial and execution of the King and the proclamation of the republic (Commonwealth), which was to last eleven years. In 1649 the split with the Levellers became complete, and they were crushed at Burford. Still there was no rest. The future Charles II invaded England at the head of a Scottish army, but in this campaign (1650) the victories of Dunbar and Worcester gave final stability to the Commonwealth. Ireland alone remained to be subdued in the war of 1651.

Two years later Cromwell accepted the office of Lord Protector. After his death in 1658, the King was recalled in 1660, but though this was always called a " Restoration," it was nothing of the kind. The new Monarchy was " limited," not feudal, i.e. a constitutional *bourgeois* capitalist monarchy. And in this sense the somewhat unconscious aims of the Parliament of 1640 were eventually achieved.

The conduct of Cromwell during the English Revolution rather resembles that of Pilsudski in recent Polish history. Pilsudski is said to have remarked that he and his friends were all travelling in a tram marked " Socialism," but that he got out at the station of " Polish Nationalism," while the others went on. In a rather similar way, Cromwell and his intimate officers were staunch radicals up to 1649. Thus in a letter to the Speaker in 1645, when Parliament was trying to persuade the soldiers to take the Presbyterian covenant, Cromwell wrote: " Honest men served you faithfully in this action. Sir, they are trusty; I beseech you, in the name of God, not to discourage them. He that ventures his life for the liberty of his country, I wish he trust God for the liberty of his conscience, and you for the liberty he fights for."

Only when the Levellers showed their determination to push the principles of Independent radicalism to their logical conclusion, did Cromwell and his officers leave the tram, by making common cause with the Presbyterian merchant party, as will be told hereafter. The personal aspect of this change is of interest mainly to biographers of Cromwell, but it is certain that he considered himself as of good birth. Thus in the House of Commons in September, 1654, he spoke as follows: " I called not myself to this place, to that God is witness, and I have many witnesses, who, I do believe, could lay down their lives bearing witness to the truth of that. I was by birth a gentleman, living neither in considerable height nor yet in obscurity." In another speech at the same time,[1] he said: " A nobleman, a gentleman, a yeoman; the distinction of these; that is a good interest of the nation, and a great one. This natural magistracy of the nation, was it not almost trampled underfoot, under despite and contempt, by men of Levelling principles? . . . Did not the Levelling principle tend to the reducing of all to an equality ? . . . What was the purport of it but to make the tenant as liberal a fortune as the landlord ? " Thus it is clear that neither the inspired prophecy of Winstanley about the classless state, nor the insistence of Lilburne on the mechanism of democracy, had had the slightest effect upon Cromwell's mind.

That early in 1649 Cromwell was exceedingly nervous regarding the power of the Levellers is shown by the fact that when Lilburne, Overton, Walwyn and Prince were imprisoned in the Tower at that time, he was heard to say to the Court with great emphasis: " You must break them, or they will break you " (*see* p. 71).

If the Parliamentary side was divided after 1646, so

---

[1] These speeches are full of indications of the importance which Cromwell attached to the activities of trade and industry under the control of the merchants.

also were the Levellers themselves, and it is interesting that their division was one between a pacifist and a military wing. By 1649 nearly all the most important regiments in the Army, under leaders like Lieut.-Colonel John Lilburne, Major-General Harrison, Colonel Rainborough, Captain Thompson, Major Wildman, Lieut.-General Tho. Hammond and others were in favour of the Levellers' programme. But there were also a number of civilian leaders, such as Gerard Winstanley and William Everard, who agitated for the setting up of what we should now call "collectivised agriculture." These latter were sometimes referred to as the "True Levellers."

Before we consider the events which took place in the Army, it will be desirable to look at the programme and activities of the True Levellers, for the best theoretical exposition of the aims of the whole movement can be found in the True Levellers' writings.

CHAPTER II

THE LEVELLERS AND THE CO-OPERATIVE COMMONWEALTH

THE DIGGERS AT COBHAM

In April, 1649, there appeared at Cobham in Surrey a number of men, armed with spades, who began to dig up the common land near or on St. George's Hill with the intention of growing corn, roots, beans and other produce. They issued, under the signatures of Winstanley and Everard, the following " *Large Declaration* " :

" That all the liberties of the people were lost by the coming of William the Conqueror and that ever since the people of God had lived under tyranny and oppression worse than that under the Egyptians. But God would bring his people out of slavery, and restore them to their freedom in enjoying the fruits and benefits of the earth. That they intend not to meddle with any man's property nor to break down any enclosures, only to meddle with what was common and untilled, to make it fruitful for the use of man. And that the time will be when all men shall willingly come in and to give up their lands and estates and submit to the community. And for those who should come and work, they should have meat, drink and clothes, which is all that is necessary to the life of man, and that for money there was no need of it, nor of clothes more than to cover nakedness. That they will not defend themselves by arms, but submit to authority, and wait until the promised opportunity be offered, which they conceive to be at hand."

After about a fortnight they were arrested by two troops of horse sent down by Cromwell, and the leaders were brought before him. It is recorded that while they were before the General they " stood in their hats,[1] and, being demanded the reason thereof, they said he was but their fellow creature." The examination showed that these True Levellers were in reality trying to found what we should now call a " collective farm," and their conviction was that when the success of the venture became clear then the mass of the population would join in and establish a national co-operative agriculture. They made that beginning on common land, claiming that from of old it had been the property of the people. News shortly came in that other groups of Levellers were beginning ventures of the same sort at Wellingborough and elsewhere, but the movement did not quickly spread. Though subject to continual interference and injuries both from Cromwell's officers and from the local landowners, the Cobham colony seems to have struggled on till the beginning of 1651.

Winstanley, however, published a number of writings, beginning with *A Vindication of Those whose Endeavour is only to make the Earth a Common Treasury, called Diggers* (1649). His theoretical beliefs appeared in his two short books, *A New Year's Gift to the Parliament and the Army, showing what the kingly power is, and that the cause of those they call the Diggers is the right and marrow of that cause that Parliament hath declared they and the Army fought for* (1650), and, two years later, *The Law of Freedom in Platform; or, True Magistracy Restored: humbly presented to Oliver Cromwell, wherein is declared what is kingly government and what commonwealth government* (1652).

Shortly after the opening of the Cobham venture, there appeared, from Gerard Winstanley's pen *A letter to Lord Fairfax and his Council of Independents; with diverse questions to the lawyers and ministry proving it an undeniable*

[1] i.e. with their hats on their heads.

equity, that the common people ought to dig, plough, plant, and dwell upon the commons without hiring them, or paying rent to any. " We understand," wrote Winstanley, " that our digging upon the common is the talk of the whole land; some approving, some disowning; some are friends, filled with love, and say the work intends good to the nation, the peace whereof is that which we seek after; others are enemies filled with fury, and falsely report of us that we have intent to fortify ourselves, and afterwards to fight against others, and take away their goods from them; which is a thing we abhor; and many other slanders we rejoice over, because we know ourselves clear, our endeavour being no otherwise, but to improve the commons, and to cast off that oppression, and outward bondage, which the creation groans under, as much as in us lies, and to lift up and preserve the purity thereof."

Winstanley asked " whether it be not a great breach of the National Covenant[1] to give two sorts of people their freedom, that is, gentry and clergy, and deny it to the rest ? I affirm, it is a high breach; for man's laws make these two sorts of people the anti-Christian task-masters over the common people; the one forcing the people to give them rent for the earth, and to work for hire for them; the other, which is the clergy, forcing a maintenance of tithes from the people. A practice which Christ's Apostles and Prophets never walked in; therefore, surely, you are the false Christs and false prophets that are risen up in these latter days."

WINSTANLEY AND THE THEORY OF SOCIALISM

Another pamphlet from Winstanley's hand was *The True Leveller's Standard Advanced, or, The state of community opened and presented to the sons of man.* This manifesto

[1] In September, 1643, Parliament had adopted the Presbyterian Solemn League and Covenant. This National Covenant officers of the New Model Army were required to sign.

struck a new note by saying in the first sentences that " The Great Creator Reason made the earth a common treasury for beasts and man." Man had become a greater slave to his own kind than the beasts of the field to him. The bands of property must be broken to pieces.

Winstanley, in his other books, went to the roots of the difficulties of society, though in a somewhat idealistic way, when he characterised buying and selling as society's root evil. " Is not buying and selling," he said, " a righteous law ? No, it is the law of the conqueror, and not the righteous law of creation. How can that be righteous, which is a cheat ? For is not this a common practice, when one hath a bad horse or a cow, or any bad commodity, he will send it to the market to cheat some simple plain-hearted man or other, and when he comes home will laugh at his neighbour's hurt, and much more. When mankind began to buy and sell, then did they fall from innocency ; for then they began to oppress and to cozen one another of their creation birthright ; as, for example, if the land belong to three persons, and two of them buy and sell the earth, and the third gives no consent, his right is taken from him, and his posterity is engaged in a war. When the earth was first bought and sold, many gave no consent. Therefore, this buying and selling did bring in, and still doth bring in, discontent and wars, which have plagued mankind sufficiently for so doing. And the nations of the world will never learn to beat their swords into ploughshares, and their spears into pruning hooks, and leave off warring, until this cheating device of buying and selling be cast out among the rubbish of kingly power." Winstanley saw far more clearly than most of his contemporaries the relation between commerce, class domination and war.

Winstanley's attitude towards religion is extremely interesting, anticipating as it did to some extent the criticism of religion as the opium of the people. Winstanley calls theology " divining doctrine " and he castigates the clergy for their acquiescence in the class structure of society. " Every day," he says, " poor people are forced to work for fourpence a day, and corn is dear. And yet the tithing priest stops their mouth and tells them ' inward satisfaction of mind ' was meant by the declaration ' the poor shall inherit the earth.' I tell you, the Scripture is to be really and materially fulfilled. You jeer at the name ' Leveller ' ; I tell you, Jesus Christ is the Head Leveller." Or again, he says : " This divining doctrine which you call ' spiritual and heavenly things ' is the thief and the robber that comes to spoil the vineyard of man's peace and does not enter at the door, but climbs up another way. They who preach this divining doctrine are the murderers of many a poor heart, who is bashful and simple, and cannot speak for himself, but keeps his thoughts to himself. This divining spiritual doctrine is a cheat; for while men are gazing up to heaven, imagining after a happiness, or fearing a hell after they are dead, their eyes are put out, and they see not what is their birthright, and what is to be done by them here on earth while they are living. This is the filthy dreamer[1] and the cloud without rain.[2] And indeed the subtle clergy do know that if they can but charm the people by their divining doctrine to look for heavenly riches and glory after they are dead, then they shall easily be the inheritors of the earth, and have the deceived people to be their servants."

If, on the one hand, Winstanley anticipated the criticisms of a religion that had made men think about a future life and so accept slavishly the evils of this, he also fully recognised the great importance of science in the service of humanity. In Winstanley's idea of religious services, science was to play a considerable part. " If the earth were set free," he said, " from kingly bondage, so that everyone might be sure of a free livelihood, and if this liberty were granted, then many secrets of God

[1] Jude 8.   [2] Jude 12.

and his works in nature would be made public, which
men do nowadays keep secret to get a living by; so that
this kingly bondage is the cause of the spreading of
ignorance in the earth. But when the Commonwealth's
freedom is established, then will knowledge cover the
earth as the waters cover the seas, and not till then. He
who is chosen minister for the year shall not be the only
man to make sermons or speeches (on the day of rest
from labour); but everyone who has any experience and
is able to speak of any art or language, or of the nature
of the heavens above or the earth below, shall have free
liberty to speak when they offer themselves and in a civil
manner desire an audience; yet he who is the reader for
the year may have his liberty to speak too, but not to
assume all power to himself, as the proud and ignorant
clergy have done, who have bewitched all the world by
their subtle covetousness and pride. And everyone who
speaks of any herb, plant, art, or nature of mankind, is.
required to speak nothing by imagination, but what he
hath found out by his own industry and observation in
trial. And thus to speak, or thus to read, the law of
nature (or God) as He has written His name in every
body, is to speak the truth as Jesus Christ spake it, giving
to everything its own weight and measure. ' Aye, but,'
saith the zealous but ignorant professor[1] 'this is a low and
carnal ministry indeed. This leads men to know nothing
but the knowledge of the earth, and the secrets of nature;
but we are to look after spiritual and heavenly things.'
I answer, to know the secrets of nature is to know the
works of God, and to know the works of God within the
creation is to know God himself, for God dwells in every
visible work or body. And, indeed, if you would know
spiritual things, it is to know how the Spirit or Power of
Wisdom and Life, causing motion or growth, dwells
within and governs both the several bodies of the stars
and planets in the heavens above and the several bodies

[1] i.e. of religion.

of the earth below, as grass, plants, fishes, beasts, birds, and mankind; for to know God beyond the creation, or to know what he will do to a man after the man is dead, if any otherwise than to scatter him into his essences of fire, water, earth and air, of which he is compounded, is a knowledge beyond the line or capacity of man to attain to while he lives in his compounded body."

This passage is particularly interesting, because in general the great scientific movement of the seventeenth century was closely associated with the simultaneous rise of capitalism. It was just about this time (1646) that the *virtuosi* such as the Hon. Robert Boyle, Dr. Thomas Willis, Dr. John Wilkins, Sir Christopher Wren and others, seeing that the old scholastic philosophies would never be overthrown by the new or experimental philosophy without co-operative enterprise, began to meet in what they called the " invisible college," the nucleus of what afterwards became the Royal Society. The early Fellows of the Royal Society were all interested even more in improving trades and husbandry than in what we should to-day call " pure science," and they were in close touch with the merchants of the city of London who encouraged science by various foundations. Gresham College, for example, where the Royal Society met in London, had been founded by one of the most outstanding financiers of the just preceding period. John Wilkins, for example, wrote in his book, *Mathematical Magic*, that " besides the great delight and pleasure there is in these mathematical or philosophical enquiries, there is also much real benefit to be learned; particularly for such gentlemen as employ their estates in those chargeable adventures of draining mines, coal pits, etc., and also for such common artificers as are well skilled in the practice of those arts." Or Robert Boyle, writing in a letter about this time, to his friend Marcombes, thus: " The other humane studies I apply myself to are natural philosophy, the mechanics, and husbandry, according to the principles of our new philosophical college, that values no need but as it hath a tendency to use. And therefore I shall make it one of my suits to you that you would take the pains to enquire a little more thoroughly into the sorts of husbandry, etc., practised in your parts; and when you intend for England to bring along with you what good receipts or choice books on any of these subjects you can procure; which I had now designed to give you a description of." But Winstanley's attitude to science shows that it was not only among the upper middle class scientists, who were the friends of the new industrialism, that an understanding of the importance of science was found. Winstanley was fully aware of the importance of the study of Nature, even though he, like many of the Fellows of the Royal Society, gave as his conscious motive the study of the works of God.

Winstanley's doctrine of freedom and his interpretation of class struggles has an extremely modern ring. For example, in the *Letter to Lord Fairfax*, he says: " First, we demand, yea or nay, whether the earth, with her fruits, was made to be bought and sold from one to another ? And whether one part of mankind was made to be a lord of the land, and another part a servant, by the law of creation before the Fall ? I affirm (and I challenge you to disprove) that the earth was made to be a common treasury of livelihood for all, without respect of persons, and was not made to be bought and sold; and that mankind, in all his branches, is lord over the beasts, birds, fishes and the earth; and was not made to acknowledge any of his own kind to be his teacher and ruler, but the spirit of righteousness only his Maker, and to walk in his light, and so to live in peace. And this being a truth, as it is, then none ought to be lords or landlords over another, but the earth is free, for every son and daughter of mankind to live free upon. . . . Secondly, I demand whether all wars, bloodshed, and misery came not upon creation when one man endeavoured to be a lord over another ? And to claim property in the earth one above another ? Your Scripture will prove this sufficiently to be true. And whether this misery shall not remove till all the branches of mankind shall look upon themselves as one man, and upon the earth as a common treasury to all, without respecting persons; everyone acknowledging the law of righteousness in them and over them, and walking in his light ? Then cast away your buying and selling the earth with her fruits. It is unrighteous, it lifts one above another, it makes one man oppress another, and it is the burden of creation."

From this passage it is clear that Winstanley, in his understanding of class exploitation, is one of the pioneers of the conception of history as the history of class struggles, and one of the first to look forward to the commonwealth of the classless state.

The following passage shows how he derived secondary miseries from the primary oppression of the people by the possessing class. " True freedom," he says, " lies where a man receives his nourishment and preservation, and it is in the use of the earth. For as man is composed of the four materials of the creation, fire, water, air and earth, so is he preserved by the compounded of these four, which are the fruits of the earth, and he cannot live without them. For take away the free use of these, then the body languishes, the spirit is brought into bondage and at length departs. Do not the ministers preach for maintenance in the earth ? The lawyers plead causes to get possession of the earth ? Doth not the soldier fight for the earth ? And doth not the landlord require rent that he may live on the fatness of the earth by the labour of his tenants ? And so from the thief on the highway to the king who sits upon the throne, does not everyone strive either by force of arms or secret cheats, to get the possessions of the earth one from another because they see their freedom lies in plenty and their bondage in poverty ? Surely, then, oppressing lords of manors, exacting landlords and tithe takers, may as well say, their brethren shall not breathe in the air, nor enjoy warmth in their bodies, nor have the moist waters to fall upon them in showers, unless they will pay them rent for it; as to say, their brethren shall not work upon the earth, nor eat the fruits thereof, unless they will hire that liberty from them. For he that takes it upon him to restrain his brother from the liberty of the one might upon the same ground restrain him from the liberty of all four, viz. fire, water, air and earth. I speak now in relation between the oppressor and the oppressed; the inward bondages of the mind, as covetousness, pride, hypocrisy, envy, fears, desperation, and madness, are all occasioned by the outward bondage that one sort of people lay upon another."

Thus here this seventeenth-century socialist clearly envisages the nationalisation of the means of production, and since industry was then so undeveloped he naturally takes the earth as the symbol of the productivity of Nature.

Some of his remarks are reminiscent of the Soviet constitution of to-day. Like that, he bases much on the saying of St. Paul, "He that will not work neither let him eat," for he says, " If any refuse to learn a trade, or refuse to work in seed time or harvest, or to be a waiter at the storehouse, and yet will feed and clothe himself with other men's labours, the overseers shall first admonish him privately; if he continue idle he shall be reproved openly before all the men by the overseers and shall be forebore with for a month after this reproof. If he still continue idle, he shall be delivered into the taskmaster's hands, who shall set him to work for twelve months or until he submit to order." Another piece of Winstanley is reminiscent of the reply of the Soviet child who was asked what would a man get " who bought a pound of potatoes for twopence and sold them for sixpence " and who answered " Twelve months " ! " If any man entice another to buy and sell, and he who is enticed does not yield but makes it known to the overseer, the enticer shall lose his freedom for twelve months, and the overseer shall give words of commendation to him who refused the enticement before all the congregation, for his faithfulness to the commonwealth's peace."

Anticipations of modern Socialism are remarkably common in Winstanley's writings. Thus in his *Law of Freedom in a Platform* he says, " Government is a wise and free ordering of the Earth, and the Manners of Mankind, by observation of particular Laws or Rules, so that all the Inhabitants may live peaceably in plenty and freedom in the land where they are born and bred." The theory of primitive communism was also adumbrated by Winstanley, for he says, " Commonwealth government may well be called the ancient of days, for it was before any other, oppressing, government crept in."

In the *New Year's Gift* there is a brilliant passage in which Winstanley urges a " revolutionary jump " : " One of your officers told me, ' What ? ' saith he, ' if we grant to everyone to have the land of England in common, we do not only destroy Property, but we do that which is not practised in any Nation in the World.' I answered, it was true; Property came in by the sword, therefore the curse; for the murderer brought it in, and upholds it by his power, and it makes a division in the Creation, casting many under bondage; therefore it is not the blessing, nor the promised seed. And what other lands do, England is not to take pattern of; for England (as well as other lands) hath lain under the power of the beast, Kingly Property; but now England is the first of Nations, that is upon the point of reforming: and if England . . . would have that honour, he must cheerfully . . . set the crown upon Christ's head, who is the Universal Love or Free Community, and so be the leader of that happy Restoration to all the Nations of the World. And if

England refuse, some other nation may be chosen before him, and England then shall lose his crown. For if ever the Creation be restored, this is the way, which lies in this twofold power. First, Community of Mankind. . . . Second, Community of the Earth. These two communities, or rather, one in two branches, is that true Levelling which Christ will work at his more glorious appearance; for Jesus Christ, the Saviour of all men, is the greatest, first and truest Leveller that ever was spoke of in the world. Therefore, you rulers of England, be not ashamed nor afraid of Levellers; hate them not; Christ comes to you riding upon these clouds; look not upon other lands to be your pattern; all lands in the world lie under darkness; so does England yet, though the nearest to light and freedom of any other; therefore let no other Land take your Crown."

In the *Declaration from the Poor Oppressed People of England* (1649), signed by many others besides Winstanley, it was said that men should endeavour to " shut out of the Creation that cursed thing called Particular Property, which is the cause of all wars, bloodshed, theft and enslaving laws, that hold the people under miserie."

The only inequality which Winstanley would admit was that of titles and honours. No doubt he thought that these would be amply sufficient incentive for co-operative effort. In his sketch of an ideal commonwealth he wrote that " As a man goes through offices, he rises to titles of honour until he comes to the highest nobility, to be a faithful commonwealth man in a parliament house. Likewise he who finds out any secret in nature shall have a title of honour given him, although he be but a young man, but no man shall have any title of honour until he win it by industry or come to it by age or office-bearing. Every man that is above 60 years of age shall have respect as a man of honour by all other that are younger." It is clearly certain now that Winstanley was the author, or one of the authors, of *A Light shining in Buckinghamshire*, which will be referred to later on with regard to the Army. Very little is known of Winstanley's life save that he was by birth a Lancashire man, and in the early years of the seventeenth century some kind of tradesman in London. When the struggle against Charles I commenced, he contributed liberally to the support of the Parliamentary army, but later he seems to have been unlucky in business and settled in the country. One day while at work, as he afterwards said, his "heart was filled with beautiful thoughts, and things were revealed to him of which he had never before heard or read, and which many to whom he related them could not believe." One of these ideas was that the earth ought to be made a common treasury for all men without distinction of person. Later on, he maintained that "the poor must first be picked out and honoured in this work, for they begin to receive the word of righteousness, not the rich which are enemies of true freedom."

The pamphlet in which he thus spoke of the poor and the rich deserves a further word. It was called *A Watchword to the City of London and the Armie; wherein you may see that England's freedome, which should be the result of all our Victories, is sinking deeper under the Norman power, as appears by this relation of the unrighteous proceedings of Kingston Court against some of the Diggers at George Hill under colour of law* (August, 1649). The title-page bears the following rather pathetic lines:

When these clay-bodies are in grave, and children stand in place,
This shewes we stood for truth and peace, and freedom in our
    daies;
And true-born sons we shall appear of England that's our mother,
No Priests' nor Lawyers' wiles to embrace; their slavery we'll
    discover.

A jury of local rich freeholders had recently fined the Diggers ten pounds each and their cattle had been injured by hired ruffians. In court the Diggers were not suffered to defend themselves. The pamphlet ends with the following appeal to the neighbouring landowner, Drake, who had summoned Winstanley and his friends : " Mr. Drake, you are a Parliament man, and was not the beginning of the quarrel between King Charles and your House ? Did you not promise liberty to the whole nation if Cavalier party were cast out'? Why now will you seek liberty to yourself and the Gentry, with the deniall of just liberty and freedome to the common people that have borne the greatest burdens ? " No answer on the part of Mr. Drake is recorded. He and his fellow J.P.'s had the following two centuries on their side.

Among his other activities, Winstanley was also, it seems, enough of a poet to write the interesting *Diggers' Song* which is contained in the Clarke Papers.

You noble diggers all, stand up now, stand up now,
You noble diggers all, stand up now,
The waste land to maintain, seeing cavaliers by name,
Your digging do disdain, and persons all defame.
Stand up now, stand up now.

Your houses they pull down, stand up now, stand up now,
Your houses they pull down, stand up now,
Your houses they pull down, to fright poor men in town,
But the gentry must come down, and the poor shall wear the
    crown.
Stand up now, diggers all.

The gentry are all round, stand up now, stand up now,
The gentry are all round, stand up now,
The gentry are all round, on each side they are found,
Their wisdoms so profound do cheat us of our ground.
Stand up now, stand up now.

The lawyers they conjoin, stand up now, stand up now,
The lawyers they conjoin, stand up now,
To arrest you they advise, such fury they devise,
The devil in them lies and hath blinded both their eyes.
Stand up now, stand up now.

The clergy they come in, stand up now, stand up now,
The clergy they come in, stand up now,
The clergy they come in, and say it is a sin
That we should now begin, our freedom for to win.
Stand up now, diggers all.

There also exists a curious little pamphlet called *The Diggers' Mirth; or, certain verses composed and fitted to tunes, for the delight and recreation of all those who Dig, or own that Work, in the Commonwealth of England.* It was published in London in 1650, i.e. after the defeat of the Army Levellers, and we may quote one verse which illustrates the pacifist leanings of the Diggers:

> But Freedome is not wonn,
> Neither by Sword and Gunn;
> Though we have eight years stay'd
> And have our moneys pay'd;
> Then Clubs and Diamonds cast away
> For Hearts and Spades must win the day.

OTHER DEFENDERS OF SOCIALIST IDEAS

The civil branch of the Levellers' movement had several theorists besides Winstanley. William Walwyn, for example, a London merchant, who frequently signed the Levellers' manifestos, although few writings under his name now exist, is known by independent witnesses to have maintained that " the world shall never be well until all things be common." He said that it would not be by any means " such difficulty as men make it to be to alter the course of the world in this thing; a very few diligent and valiant spirits may turn the world upside down if they observe the seasons and shall with life and courage engage accordingly." To the objection that this would upset all and every government he answered, " There would then be less need of government; for then there would be no thieves, no covetous persons, no deceit and abuse of one another, and so no need of government. If any difference do fall out, take a cobbler from his seat, or any other tradesman that is an honest and just man, and let him hear the case and determine the same, and then again betake himself to his work." It is remarkable how these ideas in seventeenth-century England anticipate the people's judges of the U.S.S.R. It is to be noted how both in Walwyn and Winstanley the existence of unjust laws and an irrational social structure are regarded as the principal origin of mental maladjustments and even of criminal acts. Walwyn was regarded by contemporaries as the Levellers' best thinker.

Another of the Levellers was Richard Overton, who is of particular interest, since he carried out in greater detail the attack on traditional religion made by Winstanley. In Overton we may recognise one of the first representatives of the schools of thought which combine rationalism and materialism with political and social radicalism. Overton doubtless believed that the doctrine of the immortality of the soul was one of the most dangerously anti-social doctrines, since it made men concentrate on a future life instead of striving to better themselves on earth. His little book, *Man's Mortality*, appeared first in 1643. The title of the final edition runs thus: *Man wholly Mortal; or, a treatise wherein it is proved both theologically and philosophically that as the whole man sinned so the whole man died; contrary to that common distinction of soul and body. With doubts and objections answered and resolved both by scripture and reason, discovering a multitude of blasphemies and absurdities that arise from the fancy of the soul.*

It is interesting that he has two lines of argument, the first derived from the Scriptures (for there was, of course, at that time no appreciation of the changes in theological thought during the history of the Hebrews), and the second from physiological and biological considerations. Neither in his book nor in the replies to it, such as *The Prerogative of Man; or, the immortality of human souls asserted against the vain cavils of a worthless pamphlet intituled man's mortality* (Oxford, 1645), was there any overt discussion of the argument that belief in immortality is the people's opium. As we have already seen, however, Winstanley gives a remarkable anticipation of Marxist views in this respect.

Perhaps the most remarkable pamphlet which the Diggers produced was *A Light shining in Buckinghamshire*, which laid down what " honest people " desire. This work carried the sub-title *A discovery of the main grounds and original causes of all the slavery in the world, but chiefly in England, presented by way of declaration to many of the well-affected in the country and all the poor oppressed countrymen of England, and also to the consideration of the present army under the conduct of Lord Fairfax* (1648). It was couched very largely in religious and Biblical phraseology, but, as has often been pointed out by writers on this period, such terminology was natural at the time, and it would have been impossible for the Levellers to have used any other form, wanting as they did to lead a great popular agitation. " What honest people desire " is " (1) a just portion for each man to live, so that none need to beg or steal for want, but everyone may live comfortably. (2) A just rule for each man to go by, which rule is to be found in Scripture. (3) Equal rights for all men. (4) A government by judges called elders elected by the people. (5) A commonwealth after the pattern of the Bible. Now, in Israel if a man were poor a public maintenance and stock was to be provided to raise him again. So would all bishops' land, forest lands, and Crown lands do in our country, which the apostate parliament looks to give one to another and to maintain the indolent thing called a king; and every seventh year the land was to the poor, the fatherless, widows and strangers, and at every crop a portion allowed for them. And mark this, poor people, what the Levellers would do for you."

Besides the Levellers, there were a number of writers

rather closely associated with them, as may be seen from the fact that Giles Calvert, who published most of the Levellers' pamphlets and whose name figures as that of a co-editor of one of the editions of the *Agreement of the People*, published their books. One of these was Peter Chamberlain, who, in his book, *The Poor Man's Advocate*, demanded the nationalisation of all Crown and Church land. This natural stock he called " the patrimony of the poor " and suggested that it should be administered by a responsible supervisor acting under a democratic constitution. Chamberlain brilliantly attacked the belief that the poor can only be brought to reason by hunger and oppressive laws and that if not kept down by force they would become insolent and rebellious. Another associated intellectual was Samuel Hartlib, who translated some of the writings of the famous Czech educationalist, Comenius, and who suggested that the State ought to be the promoter of industry. In his *Description of the Famous Kingdom of Macaria*, showing " its excellent government wherein the inhabitants live in great prosperity, health and happiness," he suggested that there should be five councils of State, devoted to agriculture, fishery, commerce and trade on land, overseas commerce and trade, and the plantations. In suggesting that the State should undertake vast commitments in both industry and science, Hartlib was indeed many years ahead of his time. He was one of those who realised the need for a scientific foundation, such as the Royal Society, but, although he lived to see that in being, his other ideas were never understood in his lifetime. Nevertheless, his association with the Levellers is important in that we see again the understanding of some of their adherents of the importance of the new applied science.

Lastly, among the numerous remarkable anticipations of modern Socialism in the Levellers' movement, even a State medical service was envisaged; as, for instance, by the lawyer John Cook (who was Solicitor-General at the trial of the King), in his *Unum necessarium; or, The poor man's cause*.

Education was another question on which the Levellers were far in advance of their times. One of the Army's chaplains was William Dell, who married Bridget Cromwell to Commissary-General Ireton, and was afterwards Master of Caius College in Cambridge. His books also were published by Giles Calvert. In his *Right Reformation of Learning* he urged vast extensions in the system of elementary schools, believing " that the universities should away with the classical gods and muses," and concentrate on the teaching of " logic and mathematics but especially arithmetic, geometry, geography, and the like, which as they carry no wickedness in them, so are they besides very useful to human society." More interesting still, he was a violent opponent of the monopoly of learning by Oxford and Cambridge, suggesting that it would be " more advantageous to the good of all the people, to have universities or colleges, one at least, in every great town or city in the nation, as in London, York, Bristol, Exeter, Norwich, and the like; and for the State to allow these colleges an honest and competent maintenance, for some godly and learned men to teach the tongues and arts, under a due reformation."

What manner of man was Dell appears from the following accusations made against him at the Restoration: " He has reported that the King and his followers were like the Devil and his angels, and has approved of the murder of the King and the taking away of the House of Lords . . . he has entrapped the gentry of the county into discourses and then given false information against them; he has declared in the public congregation that he had rather hear a plain country man speak in the church, that came from the plough, than the best orthodox minister that was in the county; upon Christmas Day last one Bunyan, a tinker, was countenanced and suffered to speak in his pulpit to the congregation, and no orthodox minister did officiate in the church that day. Since the restoration of the expelled members of Parliament he has declared that the power was now in the hands of the wicked, and that the land was like to be flowed over again with Popery; he has put forth several seditious books, and before the horrid murder of the late King he declared publicly to his congregation that the King was no king to him; Christ was his King; Venice and Holland were without earthly kings; why might not we be without ? and that he did not approve of earthly kings."

The appeal to Venice and Holland is fairly often found in Commonwealth republican writings; it is reminiscent of the socialist's appeal to the U.S.S.R. as a going concern to-day.

CHAPTER III

REVOLUTIONARY PROPAGANDA

THE PAMPHLET CAMPAIGN

IN THE YEAR WHEN the fighting began, 1642, the Parliament opened a propaganda campaign. It started by reprinting some old writings, particularly those which had been directed in the previous century by Protestant theologians against rulers of opposite persuasions. There had long been a tradition that Christian men had the duty of rebelling against un-Christian princes, and so the *Short Treatise on Politique Power* of John Ponnet, once Bishop of Winchester, which had first been published in the reign of Queen Mary, 1556, was now reprinted.

When the Parliamentary movement later on split into the conservative Presbyterians and the radical Independents, and when later still the right-wing Independents, led by Cromwell, combined with the Presbyterian City merchants against the Independents' left wing, the Levellers, these proceedings were always accompanied by a stream of pamphlets, often anonymous, but frequently very trenchant. We have already seen examples, and later, in connection with the Army movement, we shall see more. There were numerous " Remonstrances," " Petitions," and " Letters," together with what would nowadays be called " minority reports," and pamphlets objecting to the Remonstrances. All these derive a good deal of their salt from the fact that the seventeenth century was England's high-water mark in the writing of prose. Sir Thomas Browne, for example, lived all through the Revolution. His religious doubt and intellectual perplexities were the counterpart of the external storm. The Parliamentary pamphleteers were, in general, however, too harassed and incoherent to be masters of their English, and Winstanley and Walwyn alone can compare with the prose of Milton. Lilburne's writings, it has been well said, read like the verbatim report of a man talking vehemently all night in an inn. In all these writings there are two noteworthy things; the incomplete development of the modern English system of paragraphing and punctuation, and the extraordinary colour and ingenuity displayed by writers in the choice of the titles of their pamphlets. Many examples are given in this book.

In 1642, simultaneously with the reprinting of Ponnet's Elizabethan trumpet-call, the democratic note was firmly sounded by two living writers (among many lesser men), John Goodwin, the Independent minister of a chapel in Coleman Street, London, and Henry Parker, a lawyer. Goodwin's learned and inspiring *Anti-Cavalierisme* justified resistance to a king who had failed to honour his obligations under the social contract, while Parker's *Observations upon Some of His Majesty's Late Answers and Expresses* laid down that " Power is originally inherent in the People."

The pamphlet war of this period is also interesting, as Haller has shown, for its place in the history of toleration. William Walwyn, with his *Power of Love* (1643) and *The Compassionate Samaritan* (1644), and Roger Williams, the American from Rhode Island, with his *The Bloudy Tenent of Persecution* (1644), stood shoulder to shoulder with John Milton, whose *Areopagitica* of 1644 became later the classical English defence of freedom of the Press, though in its own time it did not attract as much attention as some of the other pamphlets. Richard Overton, too, entered the fight with *The Arraignement of Mr. Persecution* (1645), who, defended by Sir John Presbyter, is prosecuted for treason by Mr. Gods-Vengeance before Lord Parliament as judge. This allegory probably gave

John Bunyan some of his ideas for the *Pilgrim's Progress*.
The Presbyterians, of course, were against toleration,
and many counterblasts were written to these demands
of the Independents for universal freedom of thought.
But we cannot see the inwardness of this fact unless we
remember that the Presbyterians were politically conservative while the Independents were radical. The plea
for toleration was only apparently a purely religious
matter; actually it involved the right to entertain dis-
turbing social and political thoughts. And it may be
noted that in fact general toleration was not granted
until more than a century later, when the middle class
was so firmly established in power that it was unthink-
able that anything could shake it.

THE LEVELLERS' NEWSPAPER

But apart from the many pamphlets published by the
Levellers, it is interesting that one of the newspapers of
the Commonwealth period may be described as their
organ. Curiously enough, this journal bore the title of
The Moderate, a title chosen, perhaps, in order to obtain
wide support. *The Moderate* was one of the first papers to
publish leading articles. *The Moderate* reproduced all the
manifestos issued by the Levellers, and drew attention
to their outstanding points in its editorials.

On August 7th, 1649, when some robbers were
executed for stealing cattle, an article in *The Moderate*
argues that many crimes originate from the institution
of private property. " We find some of these felons," said
the article," "to be very civil men, and say, that if they
could have had any reasonable subsistence by friends,
or otherwise, they should never have taken such neces-
sitous courses for support of their wives and families.
From whence many honest people do endeavour to
argue, that there is nothing but property that is the laws
of all men's lives in this condition, they being necessitated

to offend the law for a livelihood; and not only so, but they argue it with much confidence that property is the original cause of any sin between party and party after civil transactions. And that since the Tyrant is taken off, and their government altered *in nomine*, so ought it really to redound to the good of the people *in specie*; which though they cannot expect it in a few years, by reason of multiplicity of the gentry in authority, command, etc., who drive on all designs for support of the old government, and consequently their own interest and the people's slavery; yet they doubt not, but in time, the people will discern their own blindness and folly."

We learn from *The Moderate* that the Levellers' movement contained in its ranks large sections of the miners, especially of Derbyshire, who were engaged in a dispute with the Earl of Rutland, and formed at one time an armed force of several thousands.

The last number of *The Moderate* appeared in September, 1649, after which, the Cromwellian censorship system being tightened up, its publication seems to have become impossible.

Its last leading article was not without fire. After describing the course of the Revolution, the writer went on: "At last Divine Providence crowned the slavish people's attempt with good success against this potent Enemy, which made them free (as they fancied) from their former Oppressions, Burdens, and Slaveries, and happy in what they could imagine, the greatest good, both for their Soul and Body. But Pride, Covetousness, and Self-Interest took the advantage of so unvaluable a benefit. And many being tempted to swim in this Golden Ocean,[1] the Burdens and Oppressions of the people are thereby not only continued but increased, and no end thereof to be imagined. At this, the people (who cannot now be deluded, will be eased, and not only styled, but really be, the original of all lawful Authority) begin to

[1] *See* pp. 51, 82 and 85.

rage and cry out for a lawful Representative[1] and such other wholesome laws as will make them truly happy. These not granted, and some old sparks being blown up with the Gales of new Dissentions, the fire breaks out, the wind rises, and if the fewel be dry and some speedy remedy be not taken for prevention, the damage thereby must be great to some, but the benefit conceived greater to all others."

This is the place to mention one of the Commonwealth's most remarkable journalists. Marchamont Needham began by editing a Royalist newspaper, *Mercurius Pragmaticus*, but in 1649 he changed sides and, after publishing a book, *The Case of the Commonwealth of England Stated*, launched a newspaper on the Parliamentary side, *Mercurius Politicus*. He may or may not deserve the opprobrium which history quite understandably awards to those who change their opinions too often, but he is of interest to us here because, almost alone among his contemporaries, he understood that he was living in the midst of a revolutionary period. In general, the protagonists in the English Civil War were determined to prove the legality of all their proceedings. This was the rock upon which Pym and Hampden stood. Nearly all Lilburne's writings took the form of violent assertions of legal right and demands for legal redress. The King's judges came off worse than Charles at his trial because they based themselves on insecure legal, rather than compelling political, grounds; and even the gentle Winstanley's communism involved an appeal to what he conceived to have been pre-Norman law.

In contrast to all this, Needham entitled his first chapter, " That Governments have their revolutions and fatall periods." He had, of course, no theory of any kind as to the origin of such great changes, and could only ascribe them to " those rapid Hurricanoes of fatall necessity, which blow upon our affairs from all points

[1] Parliament.

of the compass." Needham was not afraid of the " power of the sword " which so greatly shocked the Presbyterians and many others whose views were not the Army's. It was a favourite argument of Cromwell's that God would not have prospered the Parliament's arms with so many abundant and overflowing mercies if the cause of Parliament had not been the Lord's. The power of the sword, said Needham, extending the argument a little maliciously, is, after all, the foundation of all governments. " If a King may thus," he wrote, " by Right of War, lose his share and interest in authority and power, being conquered, then on the other side, by right of war, the whole must needs reside in that Part of the People which prevailed over him, there being no middle power to make any claim: and so the consequence is clear likewise, that the whole Right of Kingly Authority being by military decision resolved into the prevailing Party, what Government soever it pleases them next to erect, is as valid *de jure*, as if it had the consent of the whole body of the people." But it might be said that the Parliament was only a remnant of those who had originally been elected. Against this Needham urged that the expelled Members " in adhering to the conquered party, even after the victory, and favouring the invaders,[1] were justly deprived of their interest, and the supreme authority descended lawfully to those members that had the courage to assert their freedoms, secure their own interest, themselves, and their adherents from future inconveniences, and take the forfeiture of those prerogatives and priviledges of the King, Lords, and secluded Commons, as heirs apparent, by the Law of Arms and Custom of Nations, to an investiture in the whole supremacy."

In the latter part of his book, Needham attacked the three parties on the right, the Royalists, Scots and English Presbyterians, and the party on the left, the

[1] The Scots.

Levellers. He claimed that monarchy was tyranny, told the Scots to mind their own business, and attempted to show that Presbyterianism was destructive of liberty. His chapter against the Levellers is more interesting. The following passage reminds us closely of the words of Engels (p. 81), though it was written by a contemporary of the Levellers and one who was, in effect, a representative of the rising middle class. " The first time the Levellers began to appear considerable," he wrote " was in the year 1647, when that memorable contest happened between the Army, and the corrupt party then prevalent in both Houses and in the City, at which time, though they did good service in helping to reduce the one, and purge the other; yet no sooner had Parliament recovered itself into a state of Innocence and Freedom, and begun to act in such a way as was conceived necessary to establish the liberties of the Nation, then these men made bold to carp at their proceedings, and crie out against them and the superior officers of the army, as perfidious, and betrayers of the publique interest, because themselves (a hot-headed rabble, and the meanest of the people) might not have it settled after their own humour."

When it came to specific arguments against the Levellers, Needham simply maintained that manhood suffrage would never give peaceful and rational elections. Democracy in that sense was an impossibility. But, moreover, " the plea for equality of right in government at length introduceth a claim for equality of estates." Here he touched the root of the trouble indeed.

As for the later history of *Mercurius Politicus*, it is of interest that Needham had no other than John Milton for a collaborator. In 1651, during the Scottish war, when the future Charles II was about to invade the country, the leading articles were certainly Milton's.

CHAPTER IV

THE LEVELLERS' MOVEMENT IN THE ARMY

THE EARLY DAYS OF THE CIVIL WAR

AFTER the failure of the King to impeach Pym, Hampden and other members of the House of Commons early in 1642, it was universally felt that the dispute could have no issue except through force of arms. One of the first to volunteer for the Parliamentary service was John Lilburne, later the greatest of the Leveller leaders. He was given a small command in an infantry regiment. All through the summer recruiting and other preparations went on and it was not until the autumn that the parties came to blows. The first serious action between the King's seasoned soldiers and the people's army went against the latter, but in the second encounter at Brentford in November, 1642, the fierce defence of the popular forces repelled the attack of the Cavaliers, and the King withdrew his army in the direction of Oxford.

At the Battle of Brentford Lilburne was taken prisoner by the Royalists.[1] He was tried and condemned in Oxford, but threats of reprisals by the Parliamentary

---

[1] The Lilburne family history illustrates the divisions of civil wars. John had two brothers: Robert, who became a Presbyterian colonel always faithful to Cromwell, and Henry, who was killed by his own men when caught trying to deliver up a Parliamentary stronghold to Royalist forces. As a young man of twenty, John Lilburne had been savagely treated by the authorities of the then Government for selling unlicensed puritan books, as described in his pamphlet *A Worke of the Beast* (1638). He was set free immediately the Long Parliament met.

authorities saved his life and the following year he was set free in exchange for certain Royalist prisoners. In the meantime in Cambridge, Huntingdon, Norfolk and the neighbouring parts, the Eastern Counties Association had been busily engaged in organising the New Model Army, and on Cromwell's recommendation Lilburne was appointed a major of cavalry. By May, 1644, Lilburne had distinguished himself so much on various occasions that he was appointed a lieutenant-colonel of Lord Manchester's Dragoons. He took part in many battles, including Edgehill and Marston Moor.

It is interesting that among the names of the members of the Cambridge Committee of the Eastern Counties Association at this time were names of families still found in Cambridge to-day, such as Almond and Spalding. They raised troop after troop of horse in the country villages, armed them with equipment from London or Lynn, and sent them off to join Colonel Cromwell's forces. One of the detachments was called the " Maiden troop " as it was armed by subscriptions from the girls of Norwich.

The confused atmosphere of these early days is well illustrated by the account of two young Royalists, the Branstons, who were riding from York to Essex in September, 1642: " In our return on Sunday, near Huntingdon, between that and Cambridge, certain musketeers started out of the corn and commanded us to stand; telling us we must be searched, and to that end must go before Mr. Cromwell and give account from whence we were come and whither we were going. I asked, where Mr. Cromwell was ? A soldier told us he was four miles off. I said, it was unreasonable to carry us out of our way; if Mr. Cromwell had been there I should have willingly given him all the satisfaction he could desire; and putting my hand into my pocket, I gave one of them twelve pence, who said, we might pass. By this

I saw plainly that it would not be possible for my father to get to the King with his coach; neither did he go at all but stayed at home till he died."

PRESBYTERIANS AND INDEPENDENTS

As the war went on, a split began to widen between the conservative Presbyterians and the radical Independents. The Presbyterians held steadily in view the possibility of compromise with the King, and, since this attitude might lead to treacheries in the field, all unreliable, i.e. conservative, elements were excluded from the New Model Army. It is important to note that at this time the soldiers whose views were more radical than those of their chiefs were not regarded as dangerous. The revolution was still in its opening stages.

We may pause for a moment to consider why the conservatives in the City were Presbyterians. It was because to interfere too radically with the organisation of the Church came near to interfering radically with the organisation of property relationships. Thus in 1641, the poet Edmund Waller, then a Parliamentarian, said in the House that although they might well restrict episcopacy, they ought not to abolish it altogether. "I look upon episcopacy," he said, " as a counterscarp or outwork; which, if it be taken by this assault of the people, and, withal, this mystery once revealed, that we must deny them nothing when they ask it thus in troops, we may, in the next place, have as hard a task to defend our property as we have lately had to recover it from the prerogative. If, by multiplying hands and petitions, they prevail for an equality in things ecclesiastical, the next demand perhaps may be the like equality in things temporal." This was the authentic voice of the rising middle class, determined to do away with feudal absolutism, but equally determined to keep the property privilege for itself. Waller went on to say: "I am confident that, whenever an equal division of lands and goods shall be desired, there will be as many places in Scripture found out which seem to favour that, as there are now alleged against the prelacy or preferment of the Church. And, as for abuses, when you are now told what this and that poor man has suffered by the bishops, you may be presented with a thousand instances of poor men that have received hard measure from their landlords." This makes us understand why the chaplains of the volunteer regiments of the city of London were all Presbyterians, and why, when in 1646 delegates from thousands of inhabitants of Buckinghamshire and Hertfordshire appeared at the Bar of the House to petition for the removal of tithes, their demand met with no support and they were sent home with the paternal injunction that they did not understand either the law of God or the law of man. The new men of property felt safer with a rigid and conservative Church organisation, of which they themselves would be the lay elders.

By this time Lilburne had fully taken sides with the Independents. On his release from prison, where he had been placed by Parliament for constant protest against Presbyterian Conservatism, he published his *England's birthright justified against all arbitrary usurpation, whether regal or parliamentary, or under what vizor soever: declaring the Parliament's present proceedings to be directly contrary to those fundamental principles whereby their actions were at first justified against the King* (1645).

Parliament had indeed abolished many institutions and impositions, but it was taking no great heed of working-class grievances. It had cancelled the monopolies granted by the King, but left intact the privileges of the great trading companies. Feudal obligations were also abolished or fell into disuse. But the rents, game laws, tithes, etc., by which the small tenants and inconsiderable families were greatly oppressed, remained as bad as before.[1]

Lilburne, knowing himself to be backed by many thousands, both in the Army and among the civilian population, was at this time audaciously asserting the absolute sovereignty of the elected representatives of the people in the House of Commons. For some months he was the object of a difference between the Lords and the Commons, the former condemning him to enormous fines and imprisoning him in the Tower, the latter not willing to agree to this and yet not quite having the courage to protect him from the Lords. When summoned to appear before the House of Lords, he steadfastly refused to answer them or to acknowledge their authority in any way. When in prison, petition after petition in his favour was presented, great demonstrations were held, and on August 1st, 1648, 10,000 of the poorer citizens of London, men and women, petitioned for his release. They were successful, but only because the Leveller movement had now reached serious proportions in the Army itself.

THE ARMY'S AGITATORS

After the Battle of Naseby in June, 1645, the King had been reduced to military impotence and the Parliamentary Presbyterians lost no time in moderating their enthusiasm for their army, regarding it as " full of whims " and remembering that a year's pay was owing to it. When they tried to lessen its influence by disbanding and distributing the regiments, officers and soldiers equally realised what was happening and made themselves an independent force. The soldiers created for their own needs the completely democratic institution called the " Agitators." The word is not met with before April, 1647, when it occurs in an address to the Generals

[1] At the same time Parliament was sharing out, with a liberal hand, confiscated estates among its deserving adherents.

by eight out of the ten cavalry regiments; it meant agent, or delegate, someone appointed to see that the regiment's wishes were carried out. It was agreed that each regiment should elect two Agitators from among the rank and file and the non-commissioned officers. These, together with two commissioned officers for each regiment, constituted the Council of the Army, which held its first meetings in the great church of Saffron Walden, Essex, in May, to consider the proposals of the Commissioners of Disbandment sent down from Parliament in London. On June 4th, 1647, a great convention of the Army was held on Newmarket Heath, near Kentford, on the borders of Suffolk and Cambridgeshire. The manifesto declared that the Army was not mercenary, but the free commoners of England drawn together and continued in judgment and conscience for the defence of their own and the people's rights and liberties. They all pledged themselves not to disband until some security was obtained that " we as private men, or other the freeborn people of England, shall not remain subject to the like oppression, injury, or abuse, as has been attempted." Six days later, on Thriplow Heath, near Cambridge, there was a still greater demonstration, 21,000 men being present. Another pledge was taken and all ranks determined to resist every cajolery which would turn them from their purpose of thoroughly freeing England. The Commissioners of Disbandment retired discomfited.

It is very important to note at this point the remark contained in the previous paragraph that about a year's pay (forty-three weeks) was owing to the Army. The Army was at this time acquiring that atmosphere of freedom which made it a few years later the most intellectually vital and the most politically conscious force in the country. In one of his retrospective speeches (April, 1657), Cromwell later recalled that he had said to Hampden in the early days of the first Civil War, that to counter men of honour one must have men of religion.

It had been true. But now in the Army of the Levellers reason and religion were to combine together. In such a process, however, the first step in seeing that all is not well with a social system is often the recognition of a serious disadvantage one suffers oneself. Thus many a soldier, who found that his pay was many months in arrear and that no provision was being made for the disabled and the widows and orphans, was led thereby to regard this as but one aspect of a greed for enrichment on the part of the merchants which we call the " rise of capitalism," but which he called the " ungodly tyranny of the Grandees and Presbyterian usurpers." It might almost be said, therefore, that what began the Army's leftward movement was a " trade union " question. We shall later see how this was solved.

THE OCCUPATION OF LONDON

The Army now began to approach London, and the Presbyterians of the City began to consider armed resistance. They organised the City militia, and in July, 1647, their apprentices broke into Parliament, prevented the admission of the Independent M.P.'s, and saw to the passing of a vote against the Army by the Presbyterian M.P.'s. Accordingly, the Army occupied the outskirts of London in the first week of August " in order to protect the Parliament," the City militia offering practically no resistance.

The conservative Presbyterians of the City and the Commons were now in serious consternation. Some old libraries still contain a copy of the *Ordinance of the Lords and Commons assembled in Parliament to enable the Committee of the Militia of London to raise, maintain, and continue* 600 *horse, for the defence and safety of Parliament, City, and parts adjacent. Saturday,* 10th *July,* 1647. But it was too late, and the trained bands of the City were quite unable during August to cope with the steadily advancing seasoned Parliamentary Army.

On Friday morning, September 17th, the City authorities tendered a prostrate submission to the Generals at Holland House, after which the Army marched "three deep through Hyde Park, into the City, with boughs of laurel in their hats." One may pause for a moment to visualise the first triumphant People's Army, the cavalry buffcoats and steel headpieces contrasting with the red uniforms and cumbersome matchlock guns of the infantry.[1] The initiative of the revolution had passed from Parliament to these grimly earnest men.

On September 10th, 1647, just about the time of the occupation of London, there appeared *The Resolution of the Agitators of the Army, concerning the prosecution of their late remonstrance and the protestation against the sitting of the late usurpers of parliamentary power in the parliament; with the reasons constraining them so resolutely to adhere to that their protestation; as they presented them to his Excellency Sir Thomas Fairfax.*

The usurpers were, of course, the Presbyterian M.P.'s, and they were accused of proceeding against the fomenters of a new war in a dangerous dilatory way. The writers spoke of their " deep sense of the blood and confusion that threatens the Nation by reason of the delays of removing the people's burdens, and clearing and securing their Rights and Freedoms," and declared that they were weary of waiting. Amongst the signatories there were many familiar names, some officers, such as Colonel Rainborough and Major Sexby, and some of the rank and file, such as Cornet Joyce, who captured the King, and Corporal Dober, whom we shall meet again.

At this time of deep division between the conservative Presbyterians and the radical Independents, a number

---

[1] As Mumford has pointed out, the beginnings of mass production may be traced in the provision of uniforms and arms for the seventeenth-century armies.

of more or less Royalist pamphlets were published containing some shrewd observations on both parties, such, for example, as *The Mystery of the two Junto's Presbyterians and Independents; or, The Serpent in the Bosom unfolded* (1647).

The author[1] showed a clear appreciation of the fact that the conservative party in the Revolution was associated with the capitalists of the city of London. " The Independent," he wrote, " groundeth his strength upon the Army, which if he can keep up, he hopes to give the law to all, and to produce that great Chymæra, Liberty of Conscience. . . . The Presbyterians have three pillars to support them, but the City is their chief foundation, with which they keep a strict correspondency, and a daily communication of councils."

The conservatives of the City also had their pamphleteers. There is one particularly amusing satire on the Levellers entitled *The Total and Final Demands already made by, and to be expected from, the Agitators and the Army; which will disband when they shall think seasonable, but not before, in all probability* (1647).

The writer pretended that the whole control of the armed forces of the nation was demanded by the council of Agitators, who intended to set up Cromwell as absolute emperor until they should think fit to dethrone him " to set up a new John of Leyden."[2]

The writer also pretended, rather in advance of events, that King Charles was to be arraigned and executed. He further suggested that the assembly of divines was to be dissolved and impeached for high treason, Presbyterianism suppressed, the Lord's Prayer, Creed, the Ten Commandments, psalm-singing, etc., utterly abolished as anti-Christian, and that " full and

[1] Almost certainly Clement Walker, as it was published by him after the Restoration in his *History of Independency*.

[2] One of the leaders in the peasant wars in sixteenth-century Germany.

free liberty be granted to all persons whatsoever to preach, baptise, dip, set up what new religions they please, and to broach any heresy, error, blasphemy, or new opinion without the least inhibition, as they do now within the Army's precincts."

The writer further suggested what was not far from the thoughts of the Levellers, that all Church lands and property of the nobility and gentry should be made the property of the State. An interesting point was that the writer hinted that all the forces in or about London were to be immediately dispersed and all the guards of the City and Parliament removed; and a new strong guard of horse and foot presently sent from the Army to secure the city and Tower of London and the Commons' House (under pretence of preventing a new war) " that so the lives, liberty, and estates both of Lords, Commons, citizens, gentlemen, etc., may be at the absolute mercy and free disposal of the Army, without the least hope of resistance." This shows that the City considered itself at this time to be in the gravest danger from the Levellers.

The pamphlet ends: " Judge what condition the King, Kingdom and Parliament are now in under the power of an Army of Lilburne's spirit and principles, who now by name desire his, Overton's, and Musgrave's[1] speedy enlargement,[2] in their last demands, who have written many treasonable and seditious pamphlets against monarchy, the power and privileges of parliament, magistrates, ministry, tithes; and labour to set up Anarchy, and so are fit chaplains for such a mutinous army." The *bourgeoisie* was evidently both frightened and furious.

---

[1] John Musgrave was a quarrelsome Cumberland man, who was connected with the fining of Royalist delinquents; it is not clear how he became associated with the Levellers.

[2] i.e. release from prison.

THE AGREEMENT OF THE PEOPLE

A very complicated situation now began to arise. In the early part of June the King had been taken into custody by a troop of dragoons headed by Cornet Joyce, an Agitator in Colonel Whalley's regiment. The King had been confined at Holmby and Newmarket, but the Agitators of the Army thought the safest place for him was London, and he was finally lodged at Hampton Court. But, instead of the intrigues ceasing, they now began in good earnest. Charles, always an adept at playing off one group against another, negotiated with the Presbyterians and Independents in turn, to the rising disgust of the rank and file and the revolutionary Levellers in the Army. This contributed greatly to the decay of Cromwell's influence over the rank and file. It was at this time that the high officers of the Army began to be called " Gentlemen Independents " or " Grandees," in distinction to the " honest substantive soldiers " and their leaders, " the Agitators."

At length the dissensions came to a head. The Agitators met and drew up a democratic republican manifesto entitled the *Agreement of the People*. This was published in numerous editions during the years of 1648 and 1649. It demanded that the supreme authority of the nation should be vested in a representative body of 400 members, elected by universal manhood suffrage.[1] Those in receipt of " wages or alms " were, however, excluded from the suffrage, but this was because a proletariat in the modern sense of the word did not exist. It was probably felt that servants would vote as their masters told them. The *Agreement* also demanded annual parliaments, the members of which were not to be eligible to sit in the

[1] It has often been pointed out that Cromwell and the Grandees, nothing if not practical men, probably thought such a suffrage, if quickly brought in, would lead to the return of a more or less Royalist parliament. They preferred a dictatorship of the *bourgeoisie*.

two succeeding parliaments. Civil servants were not to be eligible and lawyers sitting in Parliament were not to practise. There were to be no coercive laws respecting religion and no religious tests. Conscientious objection to military or naval service should be respected. All tolls, taxes and tithes were to be abolished within a short, fixed period and be replaced by a direct tax on every pound's worth of real and personal estate. All privilege was to be cancelled and the national militia was to take the place of the standing Army, the decision as to war resting with Parliament. Measures were to be taken to ensure work for the poor, a decent maintenance for the aged, and adequate medical provision for the sick. In his pamphlet, *England's New Chains discovered*, which was a commentary on the *Agreement*, Lilburne said that the Levellers were " resolved to take away all known and burdensome grievances, and they have also in mind to provide work and comfortable maintenance for all sorts of poor, aged and impotent people." The first editions of the *Agreement* were condemned by Parliament, as were other pamphlets produced by the Army, such as *The Case of the Army*.

Not a few pamphlets were published attacking the *Agreement*. For example, in 1648, one William Ashurst, Esq., published *Reasons against Agreement with a little printed paper, intituled Foundations of Freedom; or, the Agreement of the People*. Ashurst had a great deal to say against religious toleration and against the restriction of the death penalty to cases of murder. He also produced a defence of tithes on the usual lines. It is rather interesting and shows, perhaps, the general temper of the time that Ashurst said practically nothing about the demands of the Levellers for greater social and economic equality. His attack had to be on other grounds. In 1647 there came the further pamphlet entitled *The Case of the Army truly stated, together with the mischiefs and dangers that are imminent, and some suitable remedies, humbly proposed by the*

*agents of five regiments of horse, to their respective regiments
and the whole army, as it was presented by Mr. Edmund Bear
and Mr. William Russell, October 15th, 1647, unto his excellency Sir Thomas Fairfax.* It demanded:

(1) That Parliament should at once be dissolved and
a new election held.

(2) That the House be purged from the King's¹
sympathisers.

(3) That the declaration of the Army upon the
occupation of London be publicly owned and approved
by Parliament.

(4) That the oppressions of the poor by excise taxes
be removed and all taxes better regulated.

(5) " That the most sad oppressions of prisoners be
forthwith eased and removed," and that trials be
expedited.

(6) That all regulations against complete religious
toleration be repealed.

(7) That tithes be abolished.

(8) That the oath of supremacy be abolished.

(9) That the taking of oaths at court be limited from
those with conscientious scruples.

(10) " That a committee of conscientious persons be
forthwith selected to consider of the most intolerable
oppressions by unjust proceedings in the law; that all
the laws might be reduced to a smaller number to be
comprised in one volume in the English tongue, that
every free commoner might understand his own
proceedings."

(11) " That all privileges and protections above the
law, whereby some persons are exempt from the force
and power thereof, to the insufferable vexation and ruin
of multitudes of distressed people may be forthwith
abrogated."

(12) " That all the ancient rights and donations

¹ i.e. the remaining Presbyterians.

belonging to the poor, now embezzled and converted to other uses, as, enclosed Commons, Alms Houses, etc., throughout all parts of the land, may be forthwith restored to the ancient public use and service of the poor, in whose hands soever they be detained."

(13) "That provision be made in an honourable way for disabled soldiers, widows, and orphans."

This was signed by the following Agitators: Robert Everard and George Sadler, from Lieut.-General Cromwell's regiment; George Garnett and Thomas Beverley, from the Commissary-General Ireton's regiment; William Prior and William Brian, from Colonel Fleetwood's regiment; Matthew Wealy, William Russell and Richard Seal from Colonel Whalley's regiment; and by John Dober and William Hudson from Colonel Riche's regiment.

Russell was one of those who presented the petition. Dober we have already met with. Was the Everard a brother of William Everard, the colleague of Winstanley?

The pamphlet ends with the following sentences: "Upon the presentation to, and serious perusal thereof by his excellency, the sum of his answer was to the effect that he judged their intentions were honest, and desired that everyone of a public spirit would be acting for the public, and that for his part he had freely ventured his life for common right and freedom, and should freely engage it again, adding further that he thought it meet it should be presented to the General Council. October 18th, 1647."

THE ARMY'S PATIENCE WEARS THIN

The *Case of the Army* was followed by *A Call to all the Soldiers of the Army, by the Free People of England; justifying the proceedings of the five regiments; manifesting the necessity of the whole army's joining with them, in all their faithful endeavours, both for removing of all tyranny and oppression* . . .

and establishing the just liberties and peace of the nation: and discovering (without any respect of persons) the chief authors, contrivers and increasers of all our miseries, especially the new raised hypocrites, by whose treacherous practices, all the just intentions and actions of the Agitators, and other well minded soldiers, have been made fruitless (1647).

The writer warned the agitators against trusting in the promises of the grandees, and said, " If ye do adventure to go to Hampton Court, beware that ye be not frighted by the word Anarchy, unto a love of Monarchy which is but a gilded name for Tyranny; for anarchy had never been so much as once mentioned among you, had it not been for their wicked end; 'tis an old threadbare trick of the profane court, and doth amongst discreet men show plainly who is for the court and against the liberty of the people. Who, whensoever they positively insist for their just freedom, are immediately flapped in the mouth with, ' O, ye are for anarchy, ye are against all government, ye are sectaries, seditious persons, troublers both of Church and state, and so not worthy to live in a commonwealth.' "

This pamphlet described the Levellers' point of view about the whole war so well that one cannot forbear quoting from it at some length.

In the beginning of the war, says the writer, " the parliament so managed it as if they intended merely to rob and spoil the people, by pilling and polling them with variety of new-devised taxes . . . which both eateth the flesh and sucketh the blood of the middle and poorer sort, and so to mould and fashion the people, to bear such heavy burdens as the King should impose upon them with the less grudging and repining. But in the very point of time, when both the parliament and the armies under Essex and Manchester, had all shamefully betrayed their trusts, and that all well-affected[1] people

---

[1] " Well-affected " was the equivalent of " patriot " in the French Revolution.

were ready to be given up in his merciless hands, naked and stripped of all their wealth and strength, even then it pleased God by undiscernable means to raise the New Model Army and put power into your hands, which we thankfully acknowledge. Ye then so faithfully, industriously, and valiantly employed, as soon curbed the pride and power of the King, and freed the land from all his cruel and bloody forces. Yet whiles ye were thus busy abroad for good, the Parliament and City do confederate, and are as industrious at home for evil; after admitting none to bear office of any trust or command, but such as would submit to the covenant and presbytery; Ordinance is brought into the House and countenanced against opinions in religion, of a more bloody and dangerous consequence than any that ever was in the Court of High Commission. A committee is appointed and exercised with most vile partiality against godly peaceable people for preaching without that deceitful clergy's ordination. The House of Lords imprison commoners at their pleasure; Larner,[1] Lilburne, Overton, Tew[2] and others, and the House of Commons approve thereof, and give up the liberties of the people. ... Until the wickedness of the House of Commons came to such a pass that they had plotted your disbanding, and thereby gave you just cause to stand upon your guard; there appeared no hope, but that we, and ye, with all who had always stood for common freedom, against both kingly, lordly, and parliamentary tyranny, should have been made the objects of their scorn, and subjects of their malice, and had ere this been delivered up as slaves into the cruel hands of the King, their master. . . . And if Cromwell instantly repent not, and alter his course, let him know also that you loved and owned, just, honest, sincere, and valiant Cromwell, that

[1] Wm. Larner was one of the Levellers' printers.

[2] Nicholas Tew was imprisoned in connection with the presentation of one of Lilburne's petitions to Parliament.

loved his country, and the liberty of the people above his life, yea, and hated the King as a man of blood; but that Cromwell ceasing to be such, he ceaseth to be the object of your love."

The call ended by exhorting the agitators to *create new officers*; to unite in an exact council with the most judicious and truest lovers of the people they could find, to establish a free Parliament which should take away immediately the burdens and oppressions from the people; and to be strong and of good courage " for the voice of necessity is the call of God."

When in the foggy November of the year 1647, the King went secretly to Carisbrooke Castle in the Isle of Wight, the Levellers believed that Cromwell and the Grandees had connived at it. The whole Army was eager to follow Lilburne. " One Lilburne throughout and more likely to give, than to receive, laws." In a Royalist pamphlet of March, 1648, *The Agitator Anatomized, or, The character of an Agitator*, the soldier was described as one who " hath continuously his sword in one hand and one of Lilburne's epistles in the other, which he takes to be the balance that must weigh all men in this world and in the world to come." Cromwell decided to test the feeling of the Army in a series of meetings, the first of which was held in the middle of November at Corkbush Fields, near Ware, in Hertfordshire. The majority of the soldiers and officers at Ware wore in their hats sea-green ribbons, the Levellers' colours, together with copies of the *Agreement of the People*. The Army was harangued not only by Lilburne, Eyre, Scot and the other Levellers' leaders, but also by Cromwell, whose eloquence proved the more formidable. Lilburne's cavalry, however, received Cromwell and Fairfax with defiant shouts, till Cromwell rode among them and with his own hands tore out their sea-green emblems and arrested fourteen of them who had been specially active. The court-martial of the Grandees passed sentence of death on three of them, and one of them, Richard Arnold, was actually executed. The whole incident, however, only suppressed the feeling of the Army, and did not abolish it. Richard Arnold's memory was cherished and the demand was constantly raised for expiation of his innocently shed blood.

THE SECOND CIVIL WAR AND THE LEVELLER-GRANDEE CONFERENCES

As soon as summer began in the following year,[1] 1648, Royalist rebellions, aided and abetted by the Presbyterians, broke out in many counties, such as Kent, Essex and parts of Wales. The fighting went on until midsummer and proved fortunate for Cromwell and the Grandees, for their brilliant victories at Maidstone, Preston, Colchester, etc., in the second half of August, 1648, restored their ascendancy. If they had been defeated, or even if this campaign (the second Civil War) had lasted longer, they would have found themselves in a very critical position. Unfortunately, some of the most important leaders of the Levellers were killed or left the Army about this time. Lilburne, for example, began to give his whole time to civilian agitation and could not be persuaded to enter the Army again. Rainborough was assassinated by the Royalists.[2]

---

[1] It should be noted how everything happened in the summer, since the bad state of roads precluded mobility in winter. The Marston Moor fight was in June, 1644, Naseby in June, 1645, the summer of 1646 saw the end of the first Civil War, and the summer of 1648 the beginning and end of the second.

[2] It is said by some authorities that the first occasion on which the Levellers' sea-green colours were used was at the funeral of Colonel Rainborough in November, 1648. Rainborough was one of the high officers of the Army who strongly sympathised with the Levellers and as such he had some time before been appointed Vice-Admiral of the Fleet, when the Fleet was in an unreliable half-Royalist condition. It may be that the sea-green colours were a reference to his naval service, but they immediately took on a political significance.

The Levellers, however, saw very clearly that mere victories of the Army conferred no durable benefits on the people, and pressed for an immediate implementation of the *Agreement*. It was settled that four representatives of the Levellers and four of the Grandees should meet to discuss the chief points of the *Agreement*. William Walwyn was one of the Leveller members. At the end of 1648, Cromwell succeeded in imposing his views on the Commission, which decided that the revised *Agreement* should not go on to Parliament for signature and subsequent circulation but should be still further considered and that only so much of the *Agreement* as Parliament deemed suitable should be circulated. When Lilburne and the Levellers saw that this was as far as they could get, they retired from the conference in January, 1649.

This conference is one of much historical interest, for, according to the reports of the debates preserved in the Clarke papers, it was here that the difference in aim between the Grandee Independents and the Levellers came most consciously to light. Apart from the Levellers the only member who had a clear and coherent view of the situation was Commissary-General Henry Ireton, Cromwell's son-in-law, and his was consciously *bourgeois* to a remarkable degree. By saying that he was against the manhood suffrage desired by the Levellers because all constitutions were primarily intended to safeguard property, he somewhat nonplussed the Leveller members and put them on the defensive. When it was argued that the soldiers had adventured their lives against the King for more than that, Ireton answered that they ought to be well content, for they would now live, not under a tyrannical and capricious ruler, but under a government controlled by those with a property stake in the kingdom, and by the fixed and certain laws that their representatives would be sure to provide. Pease thinks that Ireton was rather naïve in so serenely advocating a class constitution, and in not seeing that democracy (of a kind) could be had without Communism. If he was abreast of his time, the Levellers were some four hundred years ahead of theirs. Ireton's candid expositions hardened the attitude of the Grandees.

The Revolution, however, was still moving left, though with diminishing speed. Popular resentment against the Presbyterian conservatives for having been connected with the Royalist rebels was so great that in December, 1648, Colonel Pride conducted his famous Purge of the Commons, excluding the Presbyterian conservative members. The " Rump " of Independents remained. John Goodwin celebrated the occasion by his *Right and Might well Met* (January, 1649).

These conferences between the Levellers and the Grandee Independents were notable for many other reasons. Thus in the earlier stages, Colonel Rainborough had made one of the most famous remarks of the time. " I think," he had said, " that the poorest he that is in England hath a life to live as well as the greatest he." And in reply to Ireton: " Sir, I see that it is impossible to have liberty but all Property must be taken away.[1] . . . If you *will* say it,[2] it must be so. But I would fain know what the soldier hath fought for all this while ? He hath fought to enslave himself, to give power to men of riches, to men of estate, and to make himself a perpetual slave."

The position of the parties at this time is well characterised by Bernstein: " When Lilburne and his friends," he said, " saw nothing but malevolence, falsehood, and self-seeking in Cromwell, there was, together with his ambition and class prejudice, a strong inclination to shape his conduct according to the possibilities of the moment and he was the practical politician *par excellence*: the Levellers were the theoreticians of the movement. They started from abstract political theories and accordingly saw facts through the spectacles of those theories;

---

[1] i.e. unless all property is taken away.
[2] i.e. the opposite.

but Cromwell, whose whole being was alien from abstract thinking, saw things as they really were at any given moment better than they. In a word, he was far superior to the Levellers as a practical politician, although they deserve the credit of having, in the course of the revolution, championed with vigour the political interests of the contemporary and future working class. So long as the fight was against the forces of the old régime, the Levellers could, and in fact did, show the way again and again, but as soon as these old forces were vanquished and the new forces proceeded to arrange matters after their fashion, the suppression of the Levellers became a political necessity. The hour of the class for which they fought had not yet struck."

January of 1649 was an exciting month. On the 20th, the *Agreement of the People* was presented to the Commons, and immediately published with the title *A Petition from His Excellency Thomas Lord Fairfax and the General Council of Officers of the Army, to the honourable Commons of England in Parliament assembled, concerning the draft of an Agreement of the People for a secure and present peace by them framed and prepared.*

Not long before, on the 4th, Parliament had passed a resolution declaring " That the people are, under God, the original of all just power; that the Commons of England, in parliament assembled, being chosen by, and representing the People, are the supreme power in this nation; that whatsoever is enacted or declared for law by the commons in parliament assembled hath force of law and all the people of the nation are concluded thereby, although the consent of the King or House of Peers be not had thereunto."

Parliament spoke, but the words were those of the Levellers.

At the end of the month Charles I was sentenced to death and executed. In February the House of Lords was abolished as useless and dangerous, and a Council of State consisting of Cromwell and other Grandees appointed. In May England was declared a free Commonwealth. But all was not quieted. In February, John Lilburne headed a deputation of London citizens in protest against the plans of the Council of State for the " suppression of disturbers of the peace " in the Army. The rank and file of the Army felt that much had been done for the rights of Parliament, but nothing for the rights of the people, and the sea-green colours were universal. New edicts against " mutineers " were constantly issued and this was the reason for Lilburne's pamphlet, *England's New Chains Discovered*. On March 1st there appeared *A Letter to General Fairfax and His Council of Officers* signed by eight soldiers, boldly setting forth the complaints of the Army against its leaders, accusing Cromwell of wishing for royal power and demanding immediate ratification of the *Agreement* on Newmarket Heath. On March 3rd they were court-martialled and expelled from the Army. When one of them, Robert Ward, was examined, " they asked what he said concerning that clause, that no oppression was removed; the King and House of Lords being taken away, the chief cause of all oppression. To which he answered, ' that it was not a taking away of the King and the House of Lords that made us free from oppression; for it was as good for him to suffer under the King as under the keepers of the liberties of England; both maintaining one and the same thing; viz., the corrupt administration of the law; treble damage for tithes, persecution for matter of conscience, and oppression of the poor.' "

The petition of March 1st, 1649, was laid before the council of officers by eight troopers, one of whom was that Richard Rumbold who was long afterwards executed after the Restoration, at Edinburgh, making his famous declaration that " he did not believe that God had made the greater part of mankind with saddles on their backs and bridles in their mouths, and some few booted and spurred to ride the rest."

APPROACHING THE CLIMAX

This and other courts-martial only convinced the Levellers that more energetic action was needed. On March 21st a new Levellers' pamphlet appeared with perhaps the most remarkable title of all, *The Hunting of the Foxes from Newmarket and Thriplow Heaths to Whitehall, by five small beagles (late of the Army); or, the Grandee-deceivers unmasked (that you may know them), directed to all the free people of England, but in especial, to all that have, and are still, engaged in the military service of the Commonwealth. By Robert Ward, Thomas Walston, Simon Grant, George Jellis, and William Sawyer,*[1] *late members of the army, who upon the 6th of March in the New Palace Yard, Westminster, were forced to ride with their faces towards their horses' tails, had their swords broken over their heads, and were cashiered for petitioning the Parliament for relief of the oppressed Commonwealth and delivering the account thereof to the General. Printed in a corner of freedom, right opposite to the Council of War, Anno Domini 1649.* The foxes, of course, were Cromwell, Ireton and the other Grandees, and the pamphlet exposed their actions when in the places mentioned they persuaded the troops to take action against Parliament, up to the time when they established themselves in Westminster. Almost simultaneously Lilburne made in *The Second Part of England's New Chains Discovered* a scathing denunciation of Cromwell and the Grandees. He demanded the immediate reconstruction of the Army Council by the election of regimental Agitators, and the implementation of the *Agreement* by Parliament.

Here is a quotation from *The Hunting of the Foxes*: " When they heard that the soldiers were about to petition in behalf of themselves and the people for whom

---

[1] Subsequently imprisoned.

they had engaged, they thereat were highly offended and enraged, and desperate motions upon it were made in their conventicle (by themselves styled the General Council); some moved for an act of Parliament, that they might have power to try, judge, condemn, and punish all such, whether of the Army or not of the Army, as should disturb them (as they now call it) by petition to the Parliament or otherwise; and upon the modest reply of one, who desired that the execution of civil affairs might be left to the magistrate, Colonel Huson[1] answered, ' We have had trial enough of civil courts, we can hang twenty before they will hang one.' And in the Lobby at the Parliament door, the said Huson breathing out bitter invectives against us petitioners, who then were waiting at the door for an answer to our petition, said thus openly, ' Oh that any of them durst come into my regiment, they should never go out; we shall never be quiet till some of them be cut off for examples, and then the rest will be quashed; there are some about this town that better deserve to be hanged than those Lords that are at their trial before the High Court '; And now the colonels, lieutenant-colonels, majors, captains, of this General Council, are moulding up to that sweet temper, in so much that about March 6th they concluded an act that it must now be death to petition, or for any country-man to talk to us concerning ours and their Freedom; this enforceth us to put you in remembrance of their former words, for out of their own mouths they are judged."

One very interesting result of Lilburne's second part of *England's New Chains Discovered*, was that the Council of State attempted to persuade their Foreign or Latin Secretary, John Milton, to write an answer to this pamphlet. But Milton, who probably very much sympathised with the Levellers' defence of personal liberty, absolutely refused and, as Gardiner says, " the

[1] Hewson.

attempt of the Council of State to harness their Pegasus ended in failure."

They took other measures. On March 27th Parliament condemned Lilburne's book as seditious, and on the following day Lilburne, together with Richard Overton, William Walwyn, and Thomas Prince, was arrested and brought before the Council. They being removed to an outer room, Cromwell was heard by them through the open door as follows: " I tell you, sir," he said, thumping on to the table as he spoke, " you have no other way to deal with these men than to break them, or they will break you; yea, and bring all the guilt of the blood and treasure shed and spent in this Kingdom upon your heads and shoulders, and frustrate and make void all that work, that, with so many years' industry, toil, and pains, you have done; and so render you to all rational men in the world as the most contemptiblest generation of silly, low-spirited men in the earth, to be broken and routed by such a despicable, contemptible generation of men as they are, and therefore, Sir, I tell you again you are necessitated to break them." Whereupon the four Leveller leaders were committed, protesting, to the Tower; a proposal to allow them bail being lost by only one vote. It was a turning-point of history.

In the *Hunting of the Foxes* there is a remarkably living personal attack on Cromwell and his officers: " Was there ever a generation of men so apostate, so false, and so perjured as these ? Did ever men pretend a higher degree of holiness, religion, and zeal to God and their country than these ? These preach, these fast, these pray, these have nothing more frequent than the sentences of sacred Scripture, the name of God and Christ in their mouths; you shall scarce speak to Cromwell about anything, but he will lay his hand on his breast, elevate his eyes, and call God to record, he will weep, howl and repent; even while he does smite you under the first rib. Captain Joyce, Captain Vernam and Major Saxby can tell you sufficient stories to that purpose. . . . No interest must now stand in the Army, that is against the interest of the officers; we must all bow to their lordships, and lay down our necks under their feet, and count it our honour that they will be pleased to tread upon us; but like worms, we must not turn again, upon pain of death or cashierment. This makes us call to mind the saying of Ireton to honest Major Cobbett of Snow Hill, who having joined with the Agitators of the Army, asked him ' if he were not deluded in the understanding; in joining with the giddy headed soldiers' and advised him ' not to run against the interest of himself and the officers.' And now we have plainly found what that interest was; it was long a forging, but is now brought forth. Formerly the Commons could pass nothing without the concurrence of the Lords. Now they dare pass nothing without the concurrence of the conclave of Officers; we were before ruled by a King, Lords, and Commons; now by a General, a Court martial and House of Commons; we pray you, what is the difference ? . . . We have not the change of a Kingdom to a Commonwealth; we are only under the old cheat, the transmutation of names, but with addition of new tyrannies to the old; for the casting out of one unclean spirit, they have brought with them in his stead seven other unclean spirits more wicked than the former, and they have entered in and dwelt there, and the last state of this commonwealth is worse than the first."

THE LEVELLERS' REVOLUTION

On April 25th the Levellers' Revolution began in earnest. A large detachment of Colonel Whalley's regiment[1] appeared in front of the " Bull," Bishopsgate,

[1] Whalley had been a captain of one of Cromwell's troops of horse in the Eastern Association Ironsides, and later one of the King's judges. His regiment was one of the first to elect Agitators, and the first to revolt under Thompson (*see* below).

London, where the colour-sergeant was quartered, and
compelled him to give up the standard to them. They
were due to leave London next day, but refused to go
until their demands were granted. Cromwell and Fairfax
immediately instituted a court-martial, where five of
the fifteen leaders were sentenced to death, and one
only, chosen by lot, was executed. He was Robert
Lockyer, a brave and pious soldier, only twenty-three
years of age, who had served from the beginning of the
struggle against the King. Here is the account of his
funeral from Whitelock's *Memorials*: "April 29, 1649.
Mr. Lockyer, the trooper who was shot to death by
sentence of the court-martial was buried in this manner.
About a thousand went before the corpse, and five or
six in a file. The corpse was then brought, with six
trumpets sounding a soldier's knell, then the trooper's
horse came clothed all over in mourning and led by a
foot man. The corpse was adorned with bundles of
rosemary one half stained in blood and the sword of the
deceased on them. Some thousands followed in ranks
and files, all had sea-green and black ribbon tied on their
hats, and the women brought up the rear. At the new
churchyard in Westminster some thousands of the better
sort met them, who thought not fit to march through the
City. Many looked on this funeral as an affront to the
Parliament and the army; others call them Levellers;
but they took no notice of any of them." During this
great political demonstration, although Lilburne and
Overton were again incarcerated in the Tower, they
could not let it pass by in silence. They sent a letter to
Fairfax saying that " it is by law fully proved that it is
both treason and murder for any general of the Council
of War to execute any soldier in time of peace by martial
law." On May 9th Cromwell held a review in Hyde
Park. Nearly the whole Army wore the sea-green colours.
He made a conciliatory speech; he promised that the
Agreement should be put into force, that there should be

no further arrears of pay, and that there should be a new
Parliament. But immediately afterwards news came from
Banbury that Captain Thompson with 200 horsemen of
Colonel Whalley's regiment had raised the sea-green
flag. In a manifesto, *England's Standard Advanced*, Thompson demanded the application of the revised *Agreement*
together with satisfaction for the execution of Arnold
and Lockyer, and threatened that if any harm came to
Lilburne and the other Levellers in the Tower, it would
be more than well avenged. On May 10th Colonel
Scroope's regiment at Salisbury went over to the
Levellers and so did nearly all the regiments of Ireton,
Harrison and Skippon. They pointed out in *The Unanim-
ous Declaration of Colonel Scroope's and General Ireton's
regiments* (Salisbury, May, 1649) that they had sold their
farms or given up their businesses in order to fight
against the tyranny of the King and bishops and would
not allow any new tyranny to arise.

After a good deal of marching and counter-marching,[1]
in which the Levellers tried to unite their forces, the
most active body was contacted at Burford by Fairfax
and Cromwell, who had proceeded by forced marches
with picked troops from London. Betrayed by a treachery, the Levellers in Burford were surprised in the
middle of the night and overwhelmed by superior
numbers. Only two squadrons were able to collect and
retire under Captain Thompson in the direction of
Northamptonshire. There they succeeded in taking the
town by surprise and joining with a train of artillery,
but the numbers of troops in surrounding districts
remaining loyal to Cromwell were fairly easily able to
overwhelm them. The Levellers captured at Burford
were confined as prisoners in the church where to this
day can be seen an inscription carved in the lead of the
font, "Anthony Sedley, Leveller, 1649." Three of the
prisoners were sentenced to death and were executed

[1] The exact routes are shown in a map given by Gardiner.

against the wall of the church.[1] Carlyle, who generally treats the Levellers in his *Letters and Speeches of Cromwell* with supercilious condescension, softens a little at Burford. "So die the Leveller corporals," he writes; "strong they, after their sort, for the liberties of England; resolute to the very death. Misguided corporals! But History, which has wept for a misguided Charles Stuart, and blubbered in the most copious helpless manner near two centuries now, whole floods of brine, enough to salt a herring fishery, will not refuse these poor corporals also her tributary sigh."

On returning to Oxford, the University conferred decorations on Fairfax and Cromwell in the midst of all kinds of festivities. Parliament officially conveyed to them the thanks of the nation, and the great merchants of the City, who had often enough execrated Cromwell and held tight the purse-strings in the face of official requirements of the Parliamentary army, celebrated early in June the overthrow of the Levellers by a splendid banquet given at Grocers' Hall in honour of Cromwell and Fairfax, now hailed as the saviours of sacred property.

It may be thought remarkable that the Levellers' rebellion in the Army collapsed so readily. One reason seems to be the strain which was put upon the organisation by the long distances that separated the bodies of troops, and the uncertain information about their feelings. Revolt was practically simultaneous in Scroope's and Ireton's regiments at Salisbury, Reynolds' at Bristol, Harrison's and Skippon's in Buckinghamshire, and the garrison of Banbury. The Banbury contingent joined the Salisbury regiment, and it was the meeting of this combined brigade with the troops from

---

[1] The names of the corporals were Church and Perkins; they were defiant to the last; though Cornet Thompson gave some signs of retracting the Levellers' beliefs. The fourth, Cornet Dean, made a complete retractation and so saved his life.

Buckinghamshire at Abingdon that Cromwell succeeded in preventing. The complete lack of any officers in the rebellion higher than the rank of Captain, other than Colonel William Eyre, who had been prominent at Corkbush Fields, but had since retired, is also very noticeable. Lilburne had long left the Army and was actually in prison, Rainborough was dead, Wildman had temporarily deserted the movement, and other sympathisers with a knowledge of strategy were far away in Scotland and elsewhere. By a chance, if that is the right word for these historical events, suitable leaders were, when it came to the point, lacking.

CHAPTER V

AFTER BURFORD

DECAY OF THE MOVEMENT

I T A P P E A R S that after the collapse of the movement in the Army, the civilian wing turned, as has so often happened to revolutionary movements in times of oppression, to other-worldly religiousness. It is tolerably certain that one of the most important origins of the Society of Friends, or Quakers, is to be found in the Levellers' movement. It is certain that Winstanley ended his life as a Quaker, and there is evidence that many of the other Levellers did so too. There is, however, another point of interest here. At the very end of the century there was a philanthropic Quaker movement which wished to better the conditions of the working class. Thus John Bellers, who was not born until 1654, made in 1695 his *Proposals for raising a College of Industry of all useful trades and husbandry*. It is not unlikely that Bellers and similar writers were influenced by the Leveller movement in the previous generation. And long afterwards, in 1817, the Radical Francis Place accidentally found a copy of one of Bellers' books when sorting out some old rubbish, and told Robert Owen that he had made a great discovery, a work advocating Owen's views one hundred and fifty years before. Thus we have a direct connection between the revolutionary Levellers and the Chartists, through which we may come down to the Labour movement of to-day.

Those Levellers who did not become Quakers were reduced at the end of the Commonwealth to plotting against the rule of the Lord Protector in conjunction with the exiled Royalists. Lilburne was the principal figure in several further Court trials, but no jury could be found to condemn him. At the end of 1649, Lilburne was so popular among the people of London that a commemorative medal was struck in honour of one of his acquittals bearing the significant inscription, *John Lilburne served by the power of the Lord and the integrity of his Jury, who are judges of law as well as of facts, October 26, 1649.* In 1652 Lilburne found himself an exile in Holland among banished Cavaliers, so that to Holland were exiled the forces both of the past and of the future. Eventually, Lilburne was a prisoner of State in Jersey and at Dover Castle, and at the end of his life he too joined the Quakers, dying in August, 1657.

From 1653 onwards, although Cromwell never accepted the title of King, and the Commonwealth continued until its end a republic in form, there was a steady persecution of the Independents and Republicans. Some, such as Major-General Harrison and General Ludlow, were exiled to their homes in the country and carefully watched; others, such as Mr. Overton or Colonel Okey or Colonel Alured, were imprisoned in the Tower, or in castles like Chepstow, where was Major John Wildman; and finally, in 1656, the tail-end of the Republicans, such as Thomas Scott and Arthur Haselrig, were excluded from their due seats in Parliament by a legal pretence.

CHAPTER VI

CONCLUSIONS:
THE STRUCTURE OF HISTORY

THE ANATOMY OF REVOLUTIONS

We have now to consider what was the significance of the Levellers' movement. The question has often been asked: What would have happened if the Levellers had won the day against Cromwell and the City, and had set up their free Commonwealth? It has been said that a kind of agrarian communism would have been instituted which would have led to a low standard of life, since science, which alone could bring about the industrial revolution, could only develop in association with the rise of capitalist economics. While it may be true that the productive level of industry would have remained low under a Commonwealth of the Levellers, nevertheless we have seen reasons in Winstanley, Hartlib, Cook and other writers for thinking that they very fully appreciated the possibilities of the new scientific movement (*see* pp. 26, 37).

In the history books of schools and colleges, the Levellers' movement is disregarded, and it is not difficult to believe that sufficient political reasons account for this. But more serious books on the seventeenth century also sometimes minimise the importance of the movement on more rational grounds. Thus Professor G. N. Clark, in his remarkable book on the seventeenth century, says that the social unrest of that time had little theory and very little in common with the Labour movements of later times. " Broadly speaking," he says, " there was no Socialism in it and no theoretical humanitarianism, no demand for a better social system and no appeal to a doctrine of what social systems owe to the individual man. It is not difficult to find passages in pamphlets of the seventeenth century which seem to belie this; but the history of ideas, as much as any other branch of history, must keep anticipations and survivals in their proper subordinate place. Its business is with breathing realities, not with embryos or ghosts. The anticipations of Socialism in the seventeenth century are embryonic, and even so they are to be found chiefly in periods of political and intellectual upheaval like the English interregnum, when, in the ferment of questionings and projects, everything was doubted, and everything, from woman's suffrage to communism, irresponsibly suggested."

It cannot be denied that the Socialism in the Levellers' Movement was of a rather embryonic character, for even Bernstein considered that the Levellers did not constitute a class movement, but rather the extreme left of the middle-class republican movement. All the same, it seems likely that the disinclination of Professor Clark to do justice to the Levellers' movement arises from the excessive scepticism which so many professional historians manifest towards any discernible structure in history. The fact of the matter is that there are innumerable parallels between the English Revolution and the French Revolution. In both cases the essential process was the same, namely, the destruction of aristocratic feudal power and the establishment of the power of the capitalist *bourgeoisie*. Hence in both cases we find the revolutionary left wing first of all powerfully aiding the middle-class finance powers in their struggle against the feudal past, and then in their turn being crushed as soon as the middle class feels itself sufficiently strong to do so. The Independents correspond in many ways to the Jacobins, and the Levellers to the followers of Hébert and Babœuf. The classical statement of the view that the Levellers carried the movement to positions which could not be permanently held, but whose temporary seizure safeguarded the main advance, is that of F. Engels, in his introduction to Marx's *Class Struggles in France*. " As a rule," wrote Engels,[1] " after the first great success, the victorious minority becomes divided; one half pleased with what has been gained, the other wanting to go still further and put forward new demands, which, to a certain extent at least, are also in the real or apparent interests of the great mass of the people. In individual cases these more radical demands are realised, but only for the moment; the more moderate party again gains the upper hand, and what has eventually been won is wholly or partly lost again; the vanquished shriek of treachery, or ascribe their defeat to accident. But in truth the position is mainly this; the achievements of the first victory are only safeguarded by the second victory of the more radical party; this having been attained, and, with it, what is necessary for the moment, the radicals and their achievements vanish once more from the stage."[2]

There is no doubt that the Levellers' movement was too early to base itself upon a large, awakened working class. The development of industrial workers had not yet begun in earnest. At the end of the seventeenth century, the country population seems to have consisted of at least 30 per cent of peasant freeholders and peasant tenants, with another 20 per cent of nobility and lesser gentry, so that a really formidable agrarian movement could hardly arise. There was still a great amount of enclosure and dispossessions to be made by the gentry of the eighteenth century before a revolutionary agrarian

---

[1] Tenses changed in this quotation.

[2] This was seen, as through a glass darkly, by a great historian who knew nothing of Marxism. " In 1653," wrote Gardiner, " Cromwell's work of striking down the opponents of puritanism had for the most part come to an end. His work of striking down those who exaggerated puritanism was now beginning."

movement could exist, and this was short-circuited in the end by the great migration into the towns and the formation of our industrial working class of to-day. The eighteenth century with its many colonial and foreign wars undertaken by capitalism in its early imperialist phase, diverted the activities of many of the most vigorous elements in the population and was sterile ground for political and social advance.

THE RESTORATION

There is no excuse for writers such as Buchan who sentimentalise about the restoration of the monarchy. Gardiner is right when he says: " With Charles's death the main obstacle to the establishment of a constitutional system was removed. Personal rulers might indeed reappear, and Parliament had not yet so displayed its superiority as a governing power to make Englishmen anxious to dispense with monarchy in some form or other. But the monarchy, as Charles understood it, had disappeared for ever. Insecurity of tenure would make it impossible for future rulers long to set public opinion at naught, as Charles had done. The scaffold at White-hall accomplished what neither the eloquence of Eliot and Pym, nor the Statutes and Ordinances of the Long Parliament, had been capable of effecting."

It has been well said that the nature of the Restoration was essentially a compromise between the old land-owning class and the new rising merchant class. There were indeed at that time " Old Royalists " (Cavaliers) and " New Royalists " (Presbyterians). Estates which had been actually confiscated by the Commonwealth were returned to their original owners, but those which had been sold in forced sales were not. Moreover, the land-owners freed themselves of all the remaining feudal duties owed by them to the Crown, giving it in return the Excise duty. In this way feudal obligations were shifted on to the rest of the nation and feudal property, which carried duties as well as rights with it, became modern private property carrying rights but no duties. The Presbyterian party did not long survive the collapse of the Independents, and was destroyed by the Cavalier Parliament of 1661.

From the point of view of wages, there can be no doubt that the Commonwealth, clearly though it lagged behind the demands of the Levellers, did do better for the working class than the feudal monarchy before it or the *bourgeois* monarchy after it. In a famous passage, Thorold Rogers wrote that " the wage assessments were far more generous during the Commonwealth than under the monarchies." In 1651 the minimal legal wages were only fourpence below the wages actually paid, though after the Restoration the magistrates went back to the old scale and prescribed three shillings a week less than was actually paid.

" The Puritans," wrote Thorold Rogers, " were perhaps stern men, but they had some sense of duty. The Cavaliers were perhaps polished, but appear to have had no feature except what they called loyalty. I think if I had been a peasant in the seventeenth century I should have preferred the Puritans."

SOCIALISM AND DEMOCRACY

The Levellers were accused by their enemies of wanting to level everything down, instead of up. This is the usual accusation brought against men who are restive under the inequalities in the distribution of the world's good things characteristic of all class-stratified societies. And it is, of course, true, that neither section of the Levellers' movement made it sufficiently clear in their propaganda that a socialist scheme of things would raise the standard of life of the vast majority. This only appears incidentally in Winstanley's writings, which had the

ascetic note almost unavoidable when religious phraseology is used, and the Army Levellers were so purely
devoted to getting a really representative House of
Commons that they said very little about what would
happen afterwards.

Everyone to the right of the Levellers, however, from
Lieut.-General Cromwell and his "gentlemen-
Independents" or "Grandees" to Roman Catholic
Royalists like Sir Kenelm Digby, fully believed in the
inescapability of class distinctions. Cromwell's own
words on this subject have already been quoted (p. 18).
The *bourgeois* officers of the Parliamentary Army were
not so different from the nobility of the other side in so
far as their attitude towards the common people was
concerned. For example, in *The Hunting of the Foxes*
there is a passage which by its incoherence bears the
marks of the haste and excitement of the time, touching
the proud bearing of the Cromwellian officers. We read
about the generals, that " being thus seated, even before
they were well warmed in their place, they began to
stomach ill the sitting of the private soldiers in council
with them; although it is well known that the actions
of the Army, were to be arranged by the council, which
was to consist of those general officers who concurred
with the Army in their then just undertakings, with two
common officers and two soldiers to be chosen for each
regiment; but a council thus modelled was not suitable
to their wonted greatness and ambition; it was somewhat of scorn to them, that a private soldier (though
the representor of a regiment) should sit cheek by jowl
with them, and have with an officer an equal vote in
that council; this was a thing that savoured too much
of the people's authority and power, and was inconsistent
with the transaction of their lordly interest; the title of
free election (the original of all just authorities) must
give place to prerogative patent (the root of all exorbi-
tant powers); that council must change the derivation

of its session and go from agreement and election of the soldiery to the patent of the officers, and none to sit there but commissioned officers like so many patentee Lords in the High Court of Parliament, deriving their title from the will of their General as the other did theirs from the will of the King; so that the difference was no other but in the change of names; here was (when at its perfection) as absolute a monarch and as absolute a prerogative court over the Army as ever there was over the Commonwealth; and accordingly this council was over-swarmed with colonels, lieutenant-colonels, majors, captains, etc., contrary to and beyond the tenor of the engagement." Thus loudly complained the revolutionary Army against the undemocratic character of Cromwell and his officers.

There was also, it seems, a rather shady financial side to the proceedings of the Grandees. After the collapse of Royalist resistance in the field, and when the Parliamentary forces were being disbanded and paid off, it was customary to offer each soldier only half of what was owing to him in arrears, and to give him a Government bond or " debenture " for the remainder. The term of this bond was " until these unnatural Wars be ended," but as it was by no means obvious when this would be, the Grandee officers began buying up the debentures at cheap rates, for instance, seven shillings in the pound, and with the documents so obtained purchasing the estates of exiled Royalists. The extent of the traffic and the unpopularity which it eventually caused was one of the factors which enabled General Monk in 1660 to arrange for the Restoration, though Army feeling was widely republican.

Most writers on this period make what is probably too sharp a distinction between the Diggers and the Army Levellers. Yet, although one movement, the two sections spoke with rather different voices. The Army Levellers' proposals, as Lindsay well says, referred solely to the creation of the initial machinery for a true political democracy, something which would truly express the popular will. They *assumed* that an equalitarian socialist State would result. This assumption could hardly have appeared so naïve then as now, although the great organs of propaganda were already present as the embryonic newspapers of the time. The Diggers, on the other hand, planted the seed of a co-operative movement in agriculture in the *hope* that it would spread to include all Englishmen and all forms of production. It might be said that the Army Levellers were too purely political and that the Diggers were not political enough.

The actual overlap between the two groups was small. Some pamphlets, such as the *Light Shining in Buckinghamshire*, were signed by men who were connected with both groups, and in other cases it looks as if certain families supplied members to both. Specific equalitarian demands, however, were at one time made by the Army, for in 1647 many soldiers were asking " that no duke, marquis, or earl should have more than £2,000 a year, and that the income of other classes should be proportionately restricted."

It was said above (p. 52) that what began the Army's leftward tendency was the reluctance of the City to liquidate the great arrears of the Army's pay. This question solved itself after Burford, since the greater part of those who before had been military Levellers were persuaded to form part of Cromwell's army for the subjugation of Ireland. The result of this campaign (1650), one of the greatest sources of the bitterness of Irish nationalism, was that much land in Ireland was given as recompense to the Levellers, who thus became the ancestors of many Anglo-Irish families. Thus the miserliness of the City was offset by an imperialistic method. There is an analogy between this circumstance and the way in which the *bourgeoisie* in the eighteenth and nineteenth centuries were constantly able to circumvent trade-union demands for increases in the standard of life, not by surrendering their own dominance or modifying the profit-making system, but by embarking on ever fresh wars of capitalist expansion. The Levellers were the first working-class champions to be tricked in this way.

There is another point of interest which arises in connection with the military radicalism of the Commonwealth. If to-day there still exist laws forbidding the approach of armed forces nearer than a certain distance from the Houses of Parliament or the City of London, is this not because of the fact that there was once an army of the left? The rising middle class had created this army, but in 1649 they could not control it. That class has suffered ever since from the nightmare of an army in which men such as Lilburne, Pride, Harrison and Rainborough could be colonels and generals. Such an army will exist again, and all this is but to say that capitalism contained from its origin the seeds of its own dissolution.

THE NATURE OF REVOLUTIONARY ARMIES

It is of particular interest to compare the revolutionary Army of the English Commonwealth with other revolutionary armies in subsequent times. One of the most striking things about it is that, unlike the disintegrated remnants out of which the Red Army was built in the Russian Revolution of 1917, it was a thoroughly victorious army. Not only had it swept the Royalist forces completely off the field, but it was consciously political, and as we have seen, at its height " more likely to give, than to receive, laws." These facts can only be understood if we realise that the Parliamentary Army was a rising social class in arms, or rather the temporary union of two such classes, the representatives of *bourgeois* property and the champions of the working masses. We

have seen how in the early stages of the Civil War determined men, however radical in their political and theological opinions, were welcomed as recruits for this
volunteer army. They provided the driving force which
alone could win the war. Nor was the radicalism confined to the men, for after the formation of the New
Model; the " Self-Denying Ordinance " of 1645, by
which Members of Parliament (except certain indis-
pensables such as Cromwell) had to resign their commissions in the Army, had the intended effect of getting
the old Presbyterian colonels with secret Royalist sym-
pathies out of the front line. Independency thus gained
control of the Army, and we have seen how many officers,
even some in high positions, were later on in favour of
the Leveller movement.

The social origin of the Army's officers merits a closer
examination. When Cromwell was recruiting his Ironside cavalry of the Eastern Association in 1643, he had
no scruples about whom he put in command of his
troops of horse. One of his letters is very well known:
" I had rather have a plain russet-coated captain that
knows what he fights for, and loves what he knows, than
that which you call a gentleman, and is nothing else.
I honour a gentleman that is so indeed." Thus the
captain of his first troop was James Berry, a clerk from a
Shropshire ironworks; Robert Swallow of the eleventh
(the " maiden " troop armed by subscription among
the girls of Norwich) was looked askance at by the
well-born; and Ralph Margery of the thirteenth was, as
Buchan says, so very plain and russet-coated that the
gentility of Suffolk would have none of him. On the other
hand, many of these early officers were country gentlemen, but almost all of the smaller sort.

When the New Model Army was organised two years
later, the social origin of its officers again attracts
attention. Denzil Holles, the Presbyterian, wrote that
" most of the colonels are tradesmen, brewers, tailors,

goldsmiths, shoemakers, and the like," but it is generally maintained that this was an exaggeration, as Firth has calculated that only 15 per cent of the officers were definitely not " gentlemen," another 60 per cent making the majority, being small country landowners. The close association of these, however, with the town merchants is the significant point. The remainder were of noble birth, but they may have had merchant connections for all that. Later on, in 1655, when the major-generals of the Army were acting as police prefects up and down the country, one of the causes of resentment worked up against them was their social origin. Thus it was said that Barkstead had been a thimble-maker and Kelsey a leather-worker.

It is interesting, moreover, to make a list of all those officers who were, at one time or another, sympathetic to the Levellers' movement or active in it. If they are compared with those officers who later on were prominent Republicans, though not Levellers, it will be seen that there is distinctly rather more " gentlemanliness " among the Republicans than among the Levellers. About the social origin of the Agitators details are extremely difficult to get, but it is probable that they were all of working-class origin. On the other hand, there were officers, such as Colonel Hewson, who had been a cobbler, and Colonel Okey, who had been a ship's chandler, who were definitely antagonistic to the Levellers.

In connection with this, it is interesting that, according to Firth, promotion to commissions from the ranks was usual in the Cromwellian army, but after the Restoration unheard of for more than a century.

In revolutionary periods " patriotic " motives often serve revolutionary aims. This was most clearly the case in the French campaigns against the interventionist armies of the reactionary Powers, as the words of the *Marseillaise* bear witness. It was also the case in the

Russian Civil War in 1918 and after, and is in Spain at the present day. But patriotic motives seem to have played little part in the English Civil War. It is true that there was great popular resentment against the King because of his believed intention to bring a large army of Irish Papists into England to help his cause. The small number that did actually come were annihilated at Nantwich in 1644. In the Scottish invasion the patriotic motive was a good deal more important when the militia of the counties (especially Cheshire, Stafford, Essex and Suffolk), as distinct from the Army proper, rallied to help in the crushing defeat of the Scots army of Royalist Presbyterians at Worcester in September, 1651. But on the whole it seems to have been less vital than in the French or Russian revolutions, no doubt because the great Powers of France and Spain were never in a position to interfere with the Commonwealth's affairs.

One of the natural characteristics of revolutionary armies is that they have what to-day we call " political commissioners," men commissioned by the headquarters of the revolutionary movement to accompany the army and to stimulate its political thought in the right direction. Thus the armies of the *sans-culottes* in France had their delegates from the National Convention. Looking at the English Parliamentary Army from this point of view, we might at first be tempted to regard the Agitators as political commissioners. But they were spontaneously elected by the rank and file to carry out the action dictated by the " feeling of the regimental meeting," not delegated from Parliament. There were, however, among the Cromwellian soldiers, men concerned to propagate political ideas, though again without central authority. These were the numerous and entirely spontaneous *preachers*, of which there were one or two in every section of infantry and every troop of horse. It cannot too often be said that in the seventeenth century the dividing line between theological and political ideas was very thin. The religious emphasis of puritanism was on the prophet, not the priest; and the innumerable military preachers, who entertained every kind of revolutionary belief, were prophets of a new social order as well as of mere changes in Church government. Those who began by finding no warrant in Scripture for bishops or priests, soon went on to consider the position of landlords from the same point of view. The insistence of the Hebrew prophets on social justice was like wine to the preaching trooper. For the first time for centuries in England men like him were doubting the literal truth of the creeds, and questioning all institutions, whether religious or civil.

We can get a vivid impression of the ferment of ideas from such documents as the broadsheet published on April 26th, 1647, and entitled *These Tradesmen are Preachers in and about the City of London; or, a Discovery of the most Dangerous and Damnable Tenets that have been spread within these few yeares, by many Erronious, Heriticall and Mechannick Spirits.* Underneath, twelve pictures showed men at their trades, such as tailoring, soap-boiling, etc., and among the " errors " the following are particularly noteworthy:

" 4. That the souls of men are mortall.

" 5. That we are only to believe the Scriptures so far as they are agreeable to sense and reason.

" 15. That Christ will destroy all governments, lawful and unlawful.

" 28. That all the heaven there is, is here on earth."

We have seen that one of the City pamphlets spoke of the danger (p. 56) of giving men liberty to " broach any heresy, error, blasphemy, or new opinion, without the least inhibition, as they do now within the Army's precincts."

Another view of the freethinking of the Army is to be had from the furious book of Thomas Edwards,

Gangraena, of 1646,[1] which purported to give a catalogue of all the heresies then current, especially in the Army, which, as a Presbyterian, he hated. The Army sectaries, he maintained, had been " guilty of horrible affronts to Authority . . . I might write a Book in Folio upon this head." " Some of the sectaries have spoken and written against the lawes of the land, both Common and Statute, as I believe neither Papists, nor any English men ever did before them." They " damn the Common Law as coming from the devill, and being the great bondage of England, the Norman yoke." They aim, " 'tis evident, at a totall change of the Laws and Customs of this Kingdom." Edwards ends his account of the political significance of the Army's freethinking by the following outburst: " How many deaths hath Lilburne, Overton, and the rest of their fellows not deserved, who have with so much violence sought the over-throw of the three Estates and the Lawes of the Kingdome, and in the stead of the Fundamentall Government . . . to set up an Utopian Anarchie of the promiscuous multitude, and the lusts and uncertaine fancies of weak people for lawes and rules; and if these audacious men and their daring books shall escape without exemplary punishment . . . I do as a Minister pronounce that the plague of God will fall upon the heads of those who are the cause of it."

But Edwards found London shortly afterwards a little too hot to hold him, and died a few years later in exile. The plague he had predicted unaccountably preferred to await the restoration of the monarchy.

The essence of the matter is contained in a striking passage from the *Gangraena*, in which Edwards described an experience of his. " The eighteenth day of

---

[1] Edwards' book provoked a great sensation, and there were many replies to it, notably, R. Bacon's *The Spirit of Prelacie yet working*, 1646, which was published by the Levellers' publisher, Giles Calvert.

November last," he wrote, "so soon as I came out of the pulpit at Christ-Church, at the very foot stood a man, gentleman-like all in scarlet,[1] a young man, but being dusk, I could not perfectly discern his countenance; he desired to speak a few words with me, so I stood still, and these were his words: ' Sir, you speak against the preaching of soldiers in the army: but, I assure you, if they have not leave to preach, they will not fight; and if they fight not, we must all flee the land, and be gone . . . these men who are preachers are the men whom God hath blessed so within these few monthes, to rout the enemy twice in the field, and to take 21 garrisons of castles and towns; and therefore I thought good to let you understand so much.' "

The question may be asked, whether the Army Agitators discussed questions of staff work (strategy and tactics) with the officers, or whether their debates in the Council of the Army were purely on political matters. It seems that they were purely political, and although we have instances in later revolutions, such as the Russian, of the over-ruling of Staff officers by political commissioners even on military or partly military questions, there is nothing to suggest that Cromwell and the Grandees ever had this factor to reckon with.

THE IMPORTANCE OF THE LEVELLERS TO-DAY

The importance of the Levellers' movement for British Socialism to-day lies in the fact that the ideals of Socialism and Communism are not, as so many people think, something of foreign origin, French or Muscovite, alien to the genius of the English people. The truth is exactly the opposite. Englishmen, in their revolution of the seventeenth century, when they became at once the horror and the admiration of all Europe, were the first

[1] As we have seen, red coats were first worn by English soldiers in the New Model Army.

to visualise, and to fight for, the co-operative socialist commonwealth. English socialists are too ignorant of their great traditions. The bolshevik with beard and bomb is a figure of straw invented and manipulated with much skill by the forces of reaction and privilege to terrify the simple-minded. The Ironside, invincible lover of liberty, stands behind the labour movement of to-day, but he is only dimly seen, and the great tradition is not made use of. Let Lilburne and Winstanley arise from their tombs and inspire as once they did the masses of the English people.

Looking back at the whole story of the Levellers' movement, we cannot but be full of admiration for the fight which they made. If no ideas are ever absolutely novel, the ancient concepts of social justice and freedom arise from time to time in new contexts which give them a freshness and a compulsion absolutely new. Even when we realise that the Levellers were condemned to failure from the outset, owing to the position of class relationships in England at that time, we cannot help having great affection for them as pioneers of thoughts, the vast grandeur of which humanity was not to appreciate for some centuries to come. The Levellers after 1650 exemplify that proud revolutionary saying that all the battles of the working class are defeats except the last. And the day will come, when England is a Commonwealth again, when Thriplow Heath, Corkbush Fields, Burford Churchyard, and St. George's Hill at Cobham will see the sea-green ensigns once again afloat upon the wind, set up there in solemn and permanent memorial of those who were among the staunchest fathers of the liberty of Englishmen, and the most inspired prophets of the co-operative social order.

BIBLIOGRAPHY

ASHLEY, M. P., " Financial and Commercial Policy under the Cromwellian Protectorate." (London, 1937.)

BEER, M., " Early British Economics." (London, 1938.)

BERENS, L. H., " The Digger Movement in the Days of the Commonwealth." (London, 1906.) A detailed account, but from the Quaker point of view.

BERNSTEIN, E., " Cromwell and Communism." (London, 1930.) The best interpretation of the Levellers' Movement. Bernstein was a well-known (revisionist) Marxist.

BUCHAN, J., " Oliver Cromwell." (London, 1934.)

CARLYLE, THOMAS, " Letters and Speeches of Oliver Cromwell." (London, 1866.) 3 vols.

CLARK, G. N., " The Seventeenth Century." (London, 1931.) A brilliant all-round survey.

—— " Science and Social Welfare in the Age of Newton." (Oxford, 1937.)

DAVIDSON, M., " The Wisdom of Winstanley the Digger." (London, 1904.) A pamphlet.

FIRTH, C. H., " The Raising of the Ironsides." *Trans. Roy. Hist. Soc.* 1901, *13*, 17.

—— " The Later History of the Ironsides." *Trans. Roy. Hist. Soc.* 1901, *15*, 1.

—— " Cromwell's Army." (London, 1902.) Full of interesting technical details, but has also a fine chapter on the Army's politics.

GARDINER, S. R., " History of the Great Civil War." (London, 1911.) 4 vols.

—— " History of the Commonwealth and Protectorate." (London, 1894.) 3 vols. Delightful reading. The perfect example of the unbiased historian, who seems sometimes as puzzled by events as the contemporaries themselves.

GOOCH, G. P. (ed. LASKI, H.), " English Democratic Ideas in the Seventeenth Century." (Cambridge, 1927.) A classic.

GRIERSON, H. J. C., " Cross-currents in English Literature of the Seventeenth Century." (London, 1929.) A valuable book, but vitiated by a complete failure to understand the economic aspect of the Revolution, which he regards only as a " sectarian turmoil."

HALLER, W., " Tracts on Liberty in the Puritan Revolution." (New York, 1934.) 3 vols. Facsimile reproductions and excellent commentary.

MERTON, R. K., "Science, Technology and Society in Seventeenth Century England." (*Osiris*, 1938.)

MORLEY J., "Oliver Cromwell." (London, 1904.)

MORTON, A. L., "A People's History of England." (London, 1938.)

MUMFORD, L., "Technics and Civilisation." (London, 1934.)

NEEDHAM, J., "Laud, the Levellers, and the Virtuosi." In "Christianity and the Social Revolution." (London, 1936.) Relates the Levellers to the history of science in the seventeenth century.

PEASE, T. C., "The Leveller Movement." (Washington, 1916.) A detailed account, written from the point of view of a non-Marxist constitutional historian. No economic or social interpretations.

PIRENNE, H., "Economic and Social History of Mediæval Europe." (London, 1936.) A short, convenient, and most stimulating book.

THOROLD ROGERS, J. E., "The Economic Interpretation of History." (London, 1888.)

WILLEY, B., "The Seventeenth Century Background." (London, 1934.) Interesting, mainly literary.

WINTRINGHAM, T. H., "Mutiny." (London, 1936.) Contains a chapter on the Army Levellers.

WOODHOUSE, A. S. P., "Puritanism and Liberty; being the Army Debates, 1647–9 from the Clarke MS." (London, 1938.) Edition of a fundamental document.

NOVELS: J. Lindsay's "1649," a novel dealing especially with the Levellers, is well worth reading, though it hardly equals J. H. Shorthouse's "John Inglesant" or R. Macaulay's "They were Defeated," both of which are about the Caroline period just preceding the Revolution.